No Mistakes

No Mistakes

Madisyn Taylor, Sunny Dawn Johnston,
and HeatherAsh Amara

Hier⊕phantpublishing

Cover design by Adrian Morgan
Cover photo by Shutterstock
Text design by Jane Hagaman

Hierophant Publishing
8301 Broadway, Suite 219
San Antonio, TX 78209
888-800-4240
www.hierophantpublishing.com

If you are unable to order this book from your local bookseller, you may
order directly from the publisher.

Library of Congress Control Number: 2013905103

Trade Paper ISBN 978-1-938289-11-8
Hardcover ISBN 978-1-938289-24-8

10 9 8 7 6 5 4 3 2 1

Printed on acid-free paper in the United States

Contents

Publisher's Introduction

We're all familiar with statements like "Everything happens for a reason," and "Behind every cloud is a silver lining." But are they truisms or just wishful thinking?

The purpose of this book is to test the validity of those ideas. And when we posed that question to a group of spiritual and self-help authors, the answer was a resounding, "There are no mistakes!" The following pages offer the proof they shared with us.

No Mistakes: How You Can Change Adversity into Abundance features true stories of personal triumph through some of the most difficult situations that life can offer. Each story focuses on a transformation from places of fear, sadness, and even despair, and recounts how this same situation ultimately led to a state of grace, an incredibly positive life change, demonstrating that there is always a gift waiting on the other side. From sickness, depression, abuse, and even death and loss, *No Mistakes* shows that through trust, strength, and perseverance, one can find joy, peace, and abundance in the end.

By sharing these stories of transformation, readers can truly see that in life—even in the painful moments—there are no mistakes, only gifts in disguise. Our hope is that these intimate stories will serve as a beacon in the darkest of times, as a reminder that everything *does* happen for a reason, and that with trust and a little bit of self-realization along the way, anyone has the power inside of them to turn adversity into abundance.

From Depression to Divinity
Finding Spirit's Guidance in an Unlikely Place

|||||||||||||||||||||||||||||||||||||||||||||||||||||||||||||||||||||||||||||||||||||||||||||||||||||||||||

MADISYN TAYLOR

|||||||||||||||||||||||||||||||||||||||||||||||||||||||||||||||||||||||||||||||||||||||||||||||||||||||||||

I remember clearly the day my life would change forever. It wasn't a car crash, an earthquake, or the loss of a loved one. The sky wasn't falling; I wasn't being fired from my job or evicted. It was simply . . . a feeling. A feeling that something was off, something was different. I was no longer the same person even from the moment before.

Little did I know at the time that this strange and peculiar feeling would be the start of a strange and peculiar illness that would be my companion for many years to come and the catalyst to my spiritual awakening. Though I wasn't consciously aware of it at the time, I desperately needed an awakening. I was too busy with the redundant routines in my life to realize just how badly I needed a change. So many people fill their days with mindless routines that lack any substance whatsoever, and I was no exception. This was my life: great boyfriend, great job, great apartment, great car. I thought I was happy and doing well. I thought I was going places. But things were about to change.

The funny feeling happened one day as I was shopping for more things I didn't need. This feeling made me stop in my tracks in the middle of the mall and gasp for breath. For a brief moment I thought I might die. Or maybe I was going crazy. I was scared enough to leave the mall and return home. But once I was safe and sound in my house, I brushed the feeling off as a fluke occurrence. Until it happened again . . . and again, and again.

Then, at twenty-five, I ended up in the emergency room thinking I was having a heart attack. I couldn't breathe, my heart was thundering, and I kept wondering if I was going to die. I didn't know there was something called a panic attack until that night in the emergency room. Once I knew that I wasn't dying and I could name what was happening to me, things got a little easier—for a while.

Little did I know that Spirit was trying to get my attention. But how could I know that if I didn't even know what Spirit was? I wasn't raised in a religious or spiritual household and had no knowledge that I was a being of light—mind, body, and spirit connected to all. My life was so void of Spirit that at the age of ten, while lying in my bed and thinking about death, I was completely overwhelmed with the thought that after death you would not be alive ever again for millions of years, for eternity. That meant no more ice cream, or friends, not even grass! I gasped and bolted upright in my bed, completely devastated by the thought. I never told anybody about this incident, but I now know it as my very first panic attack.

After identifying my panic attacks as an adult, I coped and went on with my life until another funny feeling came over me one day. This feeling was different though, and it left me completely and utterly void of physical energy. Day after day I lay in bed assuming I had a flu that kept hanging on. It was a strange illness; one day I would feel OK, and the next I would be bed-bound again. I had low-grade fevers and odd aches and pains, but what became most disturbing were the strange cognitive problems that started to occur.

I found myself going on the doctor tour: how many different doctors can I visit, and how many different tests can I have before I finally get a satisfactory answer? The bills and tests were endless—blood work, EKGs, EEGs, MRIs, and so on. At my worst point, I couldn't even get out of bed at all and my husband, who was then my boyfriend, had to carry me to the bathroom. The doctors told me I had chronic fatigue syndrome, which to me was a non-answer. There was no "cure."

My days became a blur. I was a blob on the sofa, unable to work or socialize. The outside world was too much for me, and when I did go out I would suffer greatly from symptoms of panic disorder and irritable bowel syndrome. From there it was easy for me to become a recluse and somewhat agoraphobic. I settled into a new routine of staying cocooned in my home and had very little contact with the outside world. But still, somewhere deep inside, I knew I didn't want to live the rest of my life like this. I just needed to find the right person to help me.

As my cognitive abilities worsened, I decided to see a neurologist who told me I was the sickest person he had ever met, but he had no idea what was wrong with me. His answer was to put me on antidepressants. I wasn't interested in taking them, as those were for people who were depressed or mentally ill and I certainly was not either of those. But I grew tired of being sick and tired, and eventually I filled the prescription. I was ready to wait the thirty days it was supposed to take for them to kick in.

It was twenty minutes later when I had another one of those strangely memorable moments. Twenty minutes after taking that first pill, I felt as if my brain woke up from a long, long slumber, almost as though it were alive for the very first time in my life! And it was with the help of this little green pill that I was finally able to start on the road to recovery.

With my brain now awake and giving me energy I was aware enough to finally start receiving and listening to the messages and nudges from Spirit. Of course I had no idea at the time that I was being guided along; I simply had "ideas" pop into my head, and, thankfully, I acted on them.

Slowly I started to crawl out of the abyss, one step at a time. The first step was listening to meditation music each day. Next, I started to devour all of the beginner books on spirituality. I found myself in utter amazement and joy as I learned that I was made of energy and I was a spiritual being of light. I wanted and needed more, and I visited the bookstore on a weekly basis, spending hours looking at books and deciding which ones I would take home.

The idea was put into my head to seek out the hands-on healing of acupuncture and energy work. It felt like coming home. I was lucky to find great people to work with who were gentle with me, almost as if they were handpicked just for my recovery. Day by day, my awareness broadened, my psychic gifts emerged, and my body healed.

It became a ten-year journey into my initial life lessons and recovery, and once I was stable enough I entered into another life cycle where I could share what I had learned with others. It was at this stage that I, along with my husband, co-founded the website DailyOM.com.

I now know what it feels like, looks like, and sounds like to get a knock at my door from Spirit. We can only learn what this "knock" is like by living it for ourselves, but once we learn to answer the door rather than wait for it to be knocked down, life becomes a little easier to navigate.

As with all things in life, the pendulum usually swings way out of balance to the opposite extreme while we are learning. For me, there was a long period of time when I assumed *everything* was a sign from Spirit. I couldn't get through a day without questioning every single thing that happened, which was overwhelming and exhausting in itself! But once I learned to pull back the reins a bit, I settled into a comfortable relationship with Spirit and soon learned exactly when to pay attention to signs I was receiving.

Years later, I still have "aha!" moments where I put together a piece of the puzzle. Things that made no sense at one time now make perfect sense, and I am blessed with a complete understanding of why something happened at that exact moment.

Illness, accidents, loss—these are our greatest teachers. If I had not become ill and spent years recovering, I would not be where I am today. If I hadn't had the courage to listen to the message and be a warrior for my well-being, I know I would be dead, either by suicide or alcoholism or drug overdose. I believe I was given an opportunity to wake up through a lengthy, arduous process. I did my homework and my footwork, I showed that I cared, and I was willing to answer the call. I didn't know it was a call at the time; I was deeply asleep. At least, that is, until Spirit slapped me upside the head and shouted, "Wake up!"

I've come out the other side and it feels good. When I think back on my life before I was an awake and aware human being, I realize that I spent most of my days going through the motions of life with little to no meaning whatsoever. I am grateful for the life-changing experience I had, as I now have a full and rich life. I recognize that I can go as deep as I want into understanding who I am and what I have to offer in this lifetime. Thankfully, I no longer need a giant thud on the head from Spirit to get my attention. I can simply stop, notice the signs, and listen for the gentle guidance of Spirit steering me toward my greatest good.

Finding Love in the Midst of Tragedy

SUNNY DAWN JOHNSTON

It was a typical Monday evening in January. My husband Brett and I were relaxing on the couch after a busy weekend of speaking events, discussing my foundation's annual charity event scheduled for the next day. I was particularly excited that my husband's best friend Jim and his girlfriend Laura would be joining us for the event. Jim was the kind of guy who lit up a room with his smile, and Laura was outgoing and fun, so I knew they would be a great asset to our fundraising endeavors.

Our conversation was interrupted at 10:20 p.m. when the phone rang. Brett looked at the caller ID and said, "Laura is calling."

My heart started to race as he got up to answer the phone. Then I heard Laura's frantic voice on the phone say, "Jim's gone."

Brett asked, "Where is he?"

Laura just repeated, "Jim's gone."

She said this at least three times as my husband continued to ask where Jim was and if he should come over and look for him. As I witnessed their exchange, I realized that Jim was dead, and he had taken his own life.

We were stunned. We sat in silence for a few minutes blindly staring into space, wondering how this could have happened, and hoping the reason why was out there. I felt shock, sadness, confusion, and pain. My body began to tremble as I thought about his boys. I took my husband's hand, and we knew we had to go over to Jim's house and help Laura.

As we headed to the car, I felt as though Jim were picking me up and moving me in that direction. Jim and Laura had recently moved into a new home so he could be closer to family and friends, and I thought about this as I clutched Brett's hand in the car.

As we turned onto Jim and Laura's street just a mile away from our own house, police cars and yellow tape surrounded the perimeter of their property. Brett pulled up to let me out, and as he was parking the car I saw Jim's parents. I immediately went to them, and as we embraced my heart broke. I could feel their emptiness, their sorrow, their pain, and their grief. I felt overwhelmed and nauseous. Then I saw Laura. Our eyes locked, and as we moved closer, I had no words.

I held her as we both cried, and I could feel the love of the archangels surrounding us.

You see, I am an angel communicator and psychic medium, and I *knew* that if there was ever a time I needed help to know how to support and guide Jim's grieving family, this was it. I called in Archangel Raphael and Archangel Michael for help. For the next three hours, we supported Laura and Jim's parents as they met with the police and coroner. After many questions, they wheeled Jim's body out of the house on a stretcher. As a psychic medium, I felt the agitation and restlessness in his spirit. I could feel the density, desperation, and heaviness of a gunshot wound. But I also felt the serenity, calm, and peacefulness of the angels' presence.

After the body was removed, Laura left, as did Jim's parents, and I went into the house to turn off the lights and lock up. As I entered the living room, chills ran down my spine. I knew this was the energy of Jim, but it did not feel like the energy I was familiar with while he was in physical form. This energy felt disturbed. As I hurried to find the front door handle in the dark, I heard these words quietly, as if whispered in my ear: "Please come back." The voice was eerie, and I quickly closed the door behind me and searched for my husband outside.

As Brett and I drove away, I could feel the pain, desperation, loss, judgment, blame, and anger—but there were also feelings of peace, relief, compassion, hope, and love. This contrast was confusing, and yet, it made complete sense. I finally settled into bed at 4:00 a.m., exhausted, as Jim's death started to really sink in. My heart ached for everyone in Jim's life—his family and friends, all of them walking their respective journeys without him. And then my thoughts went to my husband. How would he handle the loss of his best friend, sailing partner, and projects buddy? My heart ached more intensely than ever before as I wondered why our Jim would choose to take his own life. I struggled with those thoughts and judgments, though I said to myself, "I know better. I am a spiritual teacher!"

The human part of me was at battle with the spiritual being within. I knew and believed that all is as it should be, and everything happens for a reason. But I was so angry! I would feel intense anger, and then, within moments, a burst of love would move through me and I would feel the presence and peaceful energy of the angels. These waves of emotion kept coming over and over again.

In the midst of this, I kept hearing the angels say, "Trust the process of life." They gently reminded me that no one can escape this physical life without serving their purpose. I heard them say, "Jim served his purpose in the physical world," and I realized this was the truth, whether I chose to believe it in this moment or not. As my eyes grew heavy and my body settled, I wondered, "Who am I to argue?"

The morning came quickly, and Brett and I woke in tears. I looked over at my husband, who is an ex-marine kind of tough guy, and in that moment I saw his vulnerability. He had just lost his closest friend, his soul brother, and as our swollen eyes met we realized this was not a horrific nightmare; this was real. The depth of grief that we were now sharing was something we had never before experienced in our nineteen years together. We rolled out of bed silently, knowing that we were about to experience one of the most painful days of our lives. As word of Jim's death spread to friends and family, I could feel the ripple effect of broken hearts. It was a somber day for all.

As I was getting myself ready for the day, I was listening to my angel's guidance and waiting for any messages about how I could proceed. After several phone calls to friends, the messages came. I heard Jim's spirit calling to me, and I shared this with Brett. He too had felt a calling of sorts, and we both knew we needed to go back to Jim and Laura's house. At a deep level, we knew we were being called to be the "clean-up crew."

I felt energetically clear about going to the house, but I was anxious. I wasn't sure what I would see. But I held on to the absolute faith and trust that I was meant to be at that house, at that time, doing what I was called to do. As we pulled into the driveway, I invoked Archangel Michael and asked him to protect me and give me the strength to do what was needed. As I got out of the car, I felt his presence surround me and comfort me as I prepared for this profound experience.

I entered the house and felt that same chilling energy from the night before. The feelings were surprising and unsettling, and I felt very uncomfortable. But I knew Archangel Michael was with me, and I kept reminding myself that I had a bigger purpose in being there. I refused to let the heavy energy stop me.

Brett joined me then and we walked down the hall to the bathroom hand in hand. When we reached the doorway we braced ourselves for what we might see or feel. It was difficult to view the place Jim had died. We stood together, crying and embracing one another through the pain for a while. Once the initial shock was over, we surveyed the bathroom and took action with very clear intentions. Brett felt guided to clean up the area in a way that would honor the man he loved like a brother, and with each rinse of the mop Brett brought closure to their earthly friendship.

We both felt as though we were being guided to create peace and serenity, but my experience was very different from Brett's. I was aware that Jim needed help in releasing his guilt and shame to move on, and I wanted to help him so his spirit could soar with the angels. I listened for my guidance, which told me to create a green fire to release the trauma that had occurred in this space, do a house clearing, and say a blessing. As the fire burned and I cleared the house, I could see and feel the presence of the angels.

Within two hours after Brett and I physically cleaned and energetically cleared the space, a sense of peace and calm came over the house. I could feel Jim thanking us for being there and cleaning up the unimaginable, and in turn we thanked him for trusting us and giving us the opportunity to honor him in his last moments on earth. It was a profound and sacred experience. We left the house exhausted, honored, and in awe of how much our lives had changed in the last twenty-four hours.

|||||||

On the way back to our house, Brett brought up that we still had a fundraiser planned for that evening, and we had to decide if we were going to cancel it or not. As I listened within and talked with Brett, we both knew that we needed community and support. Jim assured us he would be there in spirit, so with devastation in the air and our spirits at the helm, we went.

We decided to dedicate all of the money raised at that evening's game to Jim's boys, and with that goal in mind we said a prayer and went off to our respective places in the arena to raise money. The tears subsided as we focused on giving and sharing, and the evening turned out to be a nice reprieve from the sober reality of the last twenty-four hours. I am also happy to say that we raised over eight thousand dollars—a record-setting amount in our book. We all echoed a thank you to Jim.

While we were at the fundraiser, Laura returned to her home. She was afraid of what she might feel and was quite anxious. She had no idea what to do with the dogs, where to stay, or whether she'd ever be able to walk into the house again. However, she was quite surprised to discover that the energy of fear, anger, and pain that she had felt the last time she was there was gone. Instead, she felt lightness and peace.

Laura didn't trust her own feelings at first, but as she settled in a bit she felt comfortable enough to stay there and sleep. In the days and weeks that followed, their house became a place where she found comfort, and although the days and nights were long, the presence of the angels and their love was everywhere.

What happened after is still a blur to me, as anyone who has walked this journey well knows. I was called to be a supportive wife, mother, and friend, and I asked Archangel Chamuel to help me see through the eyes of love, share this love with others, and comfort those in pain. I also called on Archangel Uriel to help me see the bigger picture. I asked to see beyond the pain to find the purpose of this experience. With the energy and support of the archangels, my role was to be love, to see love, and to believe in love so that everyone could be brought together in love.

"We gather together today to celebrate the life of a man we all loved." These were the first words I uttered at Jim's funeral. I was asked to officiate his service, and as we listened to story after story highlighting the greatness of this man, I was honored to witness the abundance of love that poured out from this adversity. We all took a breath as we realized that divine intervention had offered us precious moments and memories with him throughout the years. Jim taught us all how to love through his boys and his life.

|||||||

Sometimes we find ourselves thrust into tragic and unexpected situations. But even in moments of great sadness we must remember that we are not alone; our angels are here to help us. With the strength and guidance of the angels, I was able to help others find some measure of peace in the sudden and devastating loss of Jim. This experience I now pass on to you. When life takes an unexpected turn, my hope is that you too will lean on the angels for guidance. This will not only help you, but may also lead you to be a source of strength and support to others in their moment of great need. Learning how to do this has been one of the biggest blessings in my life.

The Journey Home

HEATHERASH AMARA

I had obviously made a huge mistake.

As I sat in my apartment in the small town of Davis, California, my critical mind picked at the already frayed edges of my self-esteem and happiness. What was I doing here? What was wrong with me that I was not making friends? Why did I think I was smart, when I was failing at English, supposedly my best subject? Where did I belong? What if I never amounted to anything?

It was my first year at college. I had spent thirteen of my eighteen years growing up in Southeast Asia. I'd graduated from Singapore American School with honors, and now I was stuck in a tiny American cow town feeling completely disconnected from everyone and everything. Was this really what I had chosen for myself?

I had wanted to go to the University of California at Davis because they had a strong equestrian program. My vision was to become an Olympic rider, a star in the fields of dressage, show jumping, and cross-country. And maybe to become a veterinarian, since Davis also had one of the best veterinary schools in the country. Despite my parents strongly encouraging me to consider more options, I refused to put in any other college applications. UC Davis was it—the golden doorway that would lead me toward my bright, successful future.

I hated it.

I had felt one spark of connection when I met a woman from Turkey in line registering for classes, and we talked about the sense of dislocation we felt in America. I noticed it everywhere; people felt hollow, and I felt that same emptiness inside myself. I took solace in being at the stables with the horses, feeling the warmth of their bodies as I buried my face in their manes and smelled the familiar barn smell that made my heart flare awake with a smile.

Despite my connection to the horses, my sense of desert emptiness continued to grow, with no oasis in sight. My new job as a late-night layout artist for the campus newspaper and a new boyfriend helped fill the space some, but they didn't erase a deep sense of longing at my core that I couldn't yet understand or resolve.

Then I discovered politics. For a year I immersed myself in activism: I marched. I protested. I fought the system. I stood up for my rights. I stood up for the rights of others. I discovered feminism, classism, racism, ageism, homophobia. I learned about wars, and corporate greed, and environmental degradation. I started writing political stories for the newspaper.

I felt powerful. My deep investment in the us-versus-them mind-set and my constant thinking about who was right and who was wrong, who was the perpetrator and who was the victim, made me feel righteously justified in being fiercely judgmental and closed off. And it filled the hole I had felt since moving to America. I was part of something important. I was a champion, a martyr. I was needed. In hindsight, I see I was a fanatic.

In December 1989 I joined a group of twelve people in a convoy of four trucks and one bus destined for Nicaragua in time for Christmas. Each vehicle was overflowing with medicine, supplies, and toys for the people of Nicaragua. Our travels took us through Mexico, Guatemala, and Honduras before we arrived at our destination, a small Nicaraguan town where a nurse from Davis ran a medical clinic.

Most of our travel was spent either waiting long daylight hours at the borders, filling out paperwork and bribing guards with toys, or doing what we swore we would not do: driving at night. At this time there wasn't yet a well-paved Pan-American Highway, and we were warned often about how unsafe it was to travel after the sun went down. So, there we were, crawling along a windy dirt road through the mountain volcanoes of Guatemala trying to make up lost time by moonlight. Our headlights had gone out. Not one to be daunted by this minor obstacle, I was leaning out the door of the rickety bus with flashlight in hand, shining light on the road ahead so our driver could distinguish solid ground from steep, unguardrailed ravine.

Four days later, on December 26, we arrived at the Nicaraguan border. The entire journey up to that point—from multiple break downs, to being delayed by border soldiers with guns, to driving at night—had been dangerous. And then we drove into a war zone.

When we entered Nicaragua, I discovered that I wasn't afraid. I was angry. At this time the Sandinistas and the Contras were at battle, and I was to hear many stories of children's schools and innocent civilians being attacked by rebels. All of the horrible stories only made me angrier. Angry that innocent people were being killed. Angry that the US government was supporting the rebels. Angry that there was war at all.

Sitting by the side of the dusty road that day, feeling war around me, I committed to die for the Nicaraguan people if necessary to help them defend their way of life. This moment was a turning point, the far swing of a pendulum I had set into motion trying to find connection and meaning.

In his book *The Five Levels of Attachment,* don Miguel Ruiz Jr. describes how at the most extreme manifestation of attachment to an idea or concept, we are willing to kill or to die for our beliefs. At a deeper level I realized that the self-righteous anger I was feeding on wasn't a result of the problems I was facing; rather, the self-righteous anger *was* the problem. I felt this truth deep in my heart, even though my mind continued to find a myriad of reasons why its cause was "right" and others were "wrong."

Almost immediately upon my return to California, I started plotting how to go back to Central America. But any time I thought about moving, I felt a message from my heart loud and clear: "You are to stay here and work with your own people." I had no idea what that voice meant; it was obviously mistaking me for someone else. My people weren't in Davis! I belonged in Nicaragua fighting the good fight, or in Asia, among people who were deeply connected to something I didn't understand. In my mind, I belonged anywhere but where I was.

Looking back, I can see that my thoughts at this time and what life had in store for me were two very different things. While my mind stayed on an old trajectory something larger was unfolding within me. Thankfully, our hearts know the path while our minds catch up.

While I tried to ignore that quiet voice in my head and listen to my heart, I also started having little glimpses beyond my own story. One day it dawned on me that what I was doing in politics wasn't working. Despite my protesting, direct action, and deep desire for change, the most tangible result I could see was that I was angry, and all of my friends were angry, too.

I started listening more to what opened me rather than reacting from my fury, which led me to the library. That summer my best friend Autumn and I carried towering armloads of borrowed books home. We spent long days ecstatically reading about earth-based spiritual traditions from around the world.

As I delved into different shamanic and native spiritual traditions, I felt like I had come home. I recognized that what I had been seeking was a connection to the Divine and a spiritual community which I had felt so deeply in the people of my beloved Asia. It wasn't something out there that I needed to attain, but something inside that needed cultivating.

Our enthusiasm for what we were reading was like a tsunami of pure joy, and Autumn and I decided we wanted to share what we were learning. We naïvely put the word out, thinking maybe ten people would show up to explore the perspective of European shamanism with us.

Except sixty people showed up to our first class. (Did I mention that at this time I was incredibly shy?) A month later a woman came into my work bubbling over about how touched she was by an article in the paper on earth-based spirituality. "I had to find the person who wrote it!" she said. I sheepishly told her I was that person. She grabbed my arm and said, "You have to teach this. When can we start?" This is how I was "drafted" by Spirit to teach.

By following the longings of my heart rather than my mind's idea of what I should be doing, I have been guided to work with many incredible teachers, including Vicki Noble, Ana Forrest, and Peggy Dylan. A dream led me to don Miguel Ruiz, where I discovered a deep alignment with the teachings of the Toltec.

Today I am blessed to work with "my people" (which I now know translates as *all* people) to help foster local and global spiritual communities and inspire individuals to reconnect to their authenticity, awareness, and innate joy. I am the mama of an amazing spirit-based organization, TOCI (The Toltec Center of Creative Intent) based in Austin, Texas. In a lovely twist of my desire to move to Central America, I take groups to Mexico and Peru to tap in to the ancient wisdom and beauty of these lands. My life is dedicated to writing and teaching and celebrating each moment. And as I look back, I know that everything that occurred on my journey was a necessary step on the path. I had to experience the depth of fanaticism so that I could ultimately overcome it to follow my heart. It's the "mistakes" such as these that I celebrate, for when we look deeper, we see that they open us to the truth that lies within every one of us.

Life Is Not What It Seems

CHRISTINE KRINKE, PhD

The sound of the rain against my bedroom window was hypnotic, and on this particular night I fell asleep almost before my head hit the pillow. I was deep asleep when suddenly something exploded into my room and landed on top of me. I screamed. The more desperately I tried to get away, the harder I kept getting knocked down, and I realized that no matter how hard I tried I could not get up. At the same time I was trying to make sense of what was happening, until eventually the back of my head was slammed into the headboard and I was in so much pain that I had to surrender.

My attacker told me to shut up or I would be killed. An intense, sharp pain brought my attention to my neck, where I felt the tip of a very large knife pressing against my throat.

A new level of fear rose inside me as I was forced into another room and onto the floor.

By now sheer terror had overcome my entire being. I was afraid to breathe, let alone fight back. My shirt was pulled over my face and I could feel my hands being bound with rope. As I lay there on the cold, hard floor my adrenaline began to wear off and the pain started to overwhelm me.

Over the course of the next several hours I was raped and beaten. I was so far beyond any level of fear or pain at that point I just wanted the nightmare to be over. I had resigned to my fate.

With that very thought, every ounce of pain vanished and a sense of peace and calmness washed over me. I felt as though I could finally breathe. With that breath came the most indescribable feeling of weightlessness, love, and compassion. I was intensely aware of the change and tried desperately to process what was happening. My arms, legs, and body seemed fine. It just didn't make any sense. Then in the midst of my confusion I heard a voice inside my head say that everything would be OK and that I was safe.

I looked around and saw angels everywhere. Below me, my body lay on the floor. I knew that body was mine, but it wasn't me—in fact, I felt totally detached from it. At some point it became clear that I was alive, but not in the sense that I was familiar with. It didn't matter that I had just been through the worst experience of my life. I was perfectly fine, surrounded by angels and more love than any one person could possibly imagine. I could feel a presence on either side of me. They had been speaking to me this whole time, trying to help me understand what was happening.

Off to the right of me the room opened up and I could see several angels standing in a group. As I wondered what was going on I was transported from where I was standing to being right in front of them. One angel stood out in front of the others and spoke to me on behalf of the group. I felt as though I knew them; they were as familiar as family or friends who had passed on, but I'd never seen any of them before in my life.

At nineteen years old, I was made aware that there was a lot that I needed to understand. Life was not really about what I believed it was. My life flashed before me, and I realized that I had been a pretty angry kid. I never wanted to be told what to do. I wanted to figure things out myself, but I was raised in a home that was like most others, where the adult told you what to do and you did what you were told with no questions asked. I felt unloved and that life was unfair. I was insecure and afraid of everything—afraid to try new things, afraid of looking stupid, afraid people would figure out I wasn't worth having around.

Up until this point, I had walled off feelings of love because I never felt like I was enough. In truth, growing up was tough. I was very strong-willed and a constant source of frustration for my parents. I often felt like my parents didn't love me, which wasn't true, but it was my reality. Feeling this way caused me a lot of pain, which eventually turned to anger. As long as I was angry, no one would want to get too close to me. And as long as no one got too close, I wouldn't have to worry about feeling the pain of not being loved.

I was able to see that my parents had gone through the same thing themselves as children, and their behavior was just part of a vicious cycle. There were generations of people thinking they weren't good enough to be loved. Wow! How sad is that? All those misunderstandings and so many people's lives affected. How different could things have been if even just one of those people had questioned what they thought was true?

The angels explained that we are loving beings and our purpose is to love—that is at the core of our being. We should love ourselves, our families, our friends—even people we do not know—because we are all one. We are connected in ways that we as humans cannot fully understand. You are me and I am you, and to be angry at you means that I also direct that anger at myself. To find fault in you means that I find fault in myself. We are not as different as we might think. We must learn to get past our fear and anger and open our hearts so that we may feel connected and loved.

I was shown what I believe was the rapist's life. I saw how mean and angry his father was. I saw how badly the rapist was treated as a boy and I saw how his mother stood by while his father beat him. I understood that if his mother interfered, it would only result in a worse beating for the boy. I could also see that the boy did not realize that his mom was doing her best to keep him safe.

I was shown how the rapist's life had become a series of

choices which kept his pain in motion, and his mind gave him permission to inflict pain on others. I felt compassion for the little boy who didn't know what love was. I felt sadness for the man who did not figure out how to break free from the cycle of pain that was his life. In short, I had been given clarity which allowed me the grace to let go of the anger I could have felt for the rest of my life for the man who changed my world that night.

As the angels were explaining the truth of love to me I began to realize how different my life could be. I understood the simple concept of intuition: if it doesn't *feel* good inside something is off; something is not matching up with you on a soul level. When something *is* right it will resonate within. I needed to learn to trust my internal truth.

We were all born with an internal truth detector that can provide the answers to all our questions if we only know how to access it. If we would learn to trust what feels right to us we would have a much easier time in our human existence. Step one is to start by learning to love yourself. After that things will begin to fall into place.

I had the most horrible and the most incredible experience of my life all in the same night. What I learned is that no matter how awful the situation, good can come from it if you are willing to see beyond that one moment in time and somehow make your way to the truth. I now have concrete knowledge of the fact that life never ends! I have learned how to let go of anger and fear and trust my internal truth. And since that night, my intuition has never lead me in the wrong direction.

We are capable of so much more than we think. Once we open our heart and learn to love, anything is possible. And as I found out, we are never alone.

A Penny from Heaven

KAREN CURRY

People say that your life can "change on a dime." Mine changed on a penny. My entire life changed in one moment when I picked up a penny in a grocery store parking lot.

At the time, I was living with a man who had proposed marriage to me several months earlier. In the name of love I moved with my four young children from my home in Arizona to his home in Minnesota.

When I moved in with him I was still recovering from the pain of my divorce a year earlier. I had gotten married at a very young age, and after seventeen years of marriage, four children, some good years, and some bitter years of fighting over finances, bankruptcy, and other stresses, moving in with a man who promised me financial support and love seemed like my dream come true.

I had been "manifesting" a soul mate for the past year. I created a list of the qualities of my ideal partner, visualized him daily, and worked hard to remove any subconscious blocks to experiencing love again. It seemed that my relationship with this man was the fulfillment of all my intentions.

I was no newbie to the concept of "deliberate creation." Over the years I had written thousands of affirmations, read every abundance book I could get my hands on, and created vision boards that covered the walls of my office. I'd experience a little magic here and there that kept me going. For example, when we'd needed a new car, my husband and I visualized the perfect vehicle and out of the blue my father-in-law gave us a beautiful red Suburban that was perfect for our large family. But by and large, I'd not seen the results I hoped for.

I knew in my heart that deliberate creation, visualizing, mind-set, positive thinking, and all that stuff worked. But soon after moving to Minnesota with the hope that things were finally turning around, I realized that I had gotten it "wrong" again. Within a few months of moving in with my boyfriend, our relationship crumbled. I was in a lot of emotional pain, barely eating, and frightened out of my mind about how to take care of my family on my own in a new town where I knew no one and had no job or source of income.

I had given up my business when I moved to Minnesota. My boyfriend had assured me that I could stay home with my kids and be a full-time mom. I had given up all my material belongings. I had no car, no furniture, no household goods, not even beds for my kids. Moving out meant the possibility of homelessness, but I had to make a change quickly.

As a mother, failing to create a better life for us was not an option. I was on my own now. My ex-husband had moved to Texas and was having his own struggles. I had the kids full-time and was exclusively responsible for our finances, and I had to get us out of the mess I had created and into something that was better for all of us.

So I started the manifesting process all over again—you know, affirmations, vision boards, visualizing—desperately hoping that this time would be different. I knew that panic would only create more chaos, so I spent a lot of time quieting my mind with meditation. I had faith that there was an elegant solution available, but I had to be still to hear it.

During meditation I was given a life-changing insight. All my life, I'd been trying to change my mind-set to make it match my desires. All of my "manifesting" had been taking place in my head, and changing the wiring in my brain ended up being rather difficult. My life experiences and conditioning had created my mind-set in the first place. But what if, instead of trying to "change" my mind, I changed my actions with the intention of reconditioning my mind? What if I could show my mind with my actions that a different outcome was possible?

I committed to taking deliberate action in all areas of my life. If magic was going to happen, I had to facilitate it. I didn't just dream about a house, I worked with a Realtor to find one even though I didn't have a penny to my name (yet!).

I applied for a mortgage even though I didn't have an income. I reopened my business even though I didn't have any clients. My life became one giant, action-packed leap of faith.

With all my years of trial and error, I was intimately familiar with the weak points in my mind-set and where my actions often fell short. There was this part of my brain that believed I wasn't "enough" to be well-loved, supported, nurtured, and successful. Even though that part of me was small and had grown smaller over the years, it was still a big enough mental monster to create a lot of "not enough" in my life. I knew that where I put my attention and focus would determine what I created in my life. If I focused on "not enough," I would get exactly that: not enough. If I was going to permanently turn my life around and support my family, the Not Enough Monster had to die.

I started vigilantly paying attention to all the places "not enough" showed up in my world. Whenever I noticed a "not enough" in any context, I immediately jumped on it, shifted my attention away from it, and refocused on my goals— which is how the penny in the parking lot marked a turning point in my life.

When I first saw that penny, I stepped over it. My arms were full. I was in a hurry. I looked at the penny and decided that it was "not enough" for me to take the time to bend down and claim it.

As soon as I heard those words "not enough" in my head, I stopped myself dead in my tracks. Here was free money. I didn't have to do anything to claim it except bend down and pick it up. If I stepped over that coin and allowed it to meta-phorically represent "not enough" in my life, I would still be allowing the not-enough mind-set to create my world.

Something magical happened when I picked up that penny. As I lifted up that coin, all of my "not enough" pro-gramming and my years of struggle were instantly erased. Deep inside of me I truly *got* that I was so much more than "not enough," and I could create from this new, unlimited perspective.

That single shift created a cascade of abundance in my life. Within two weeks, I made an offer to buy a house, and against all odds, I was given a mortgage. Out of the blue, I received a check for $17,000, which I used to buy my house. I moved into my new house with no furniture. Within a month I had so much furniture I had to have a garage sale. I reopened my business and immediately began making more money than I had ever made in my life.

After years of diligently working to change my mind-set, the simple act of bending down and letting a coin represent "more than enough" helped me make a critical shift that changed my subconscious programming and created radical transformation in my life.

I sometimes joke that I'm a twenty-year overnight success. Success often looks like it occurs overnight. But real mastery takes disciplined practice, action, and time. In theory, instant success is possible. But for most of us, the path to success is a journey marked by experimentation, necessary mistakes, and perfect practice.

Obviously, it wasn't really the penny that changed my life. Every step of my journey was instrumental in creating the momentum necessary to rewrite my mental programming. I had never made a mistake, screwed up, or been a loser, as I had secretly suspected. Every single experience of "failure" was a lesson that deepened my awareness of my unlimited creative potential.

My new perspective taught me that there are no accidents or mistakes. Bumps in the road actually serve as catalysts for growth and evolution if we can see the lessons in them, and life gives us ample opportunities to fine-tune and master the creative process. To make real change we have to embrace the lessons rather than punish ourselves for not getting it "right," take giant leaps of faith, and keep picking up the pennies from heaven.

Beneath the Surface

TIANNA ROSER

I would have given anything to have a full head of hair again. How many hours of my life had I wasted complaining about these silly strings dangling from my head? When I was younger, I wanted it curlier. Years later, it wasn't straight enough. How much time had I spent washing, drying, and styling it?

From an early age, my hair began to exert a mysterious influence over me. My first attempt at cutting my own bangs at age seven ended in tears. They were crooked, but it seemed like an easy fix. Just take a little bit off the left side. No, wait, now the right side was too long. Just a trim there and then they'd be even . . . This went on until I realized I was running out of hair to work with. After that debacle, I let my mom be in charge of any hair modifications. I was so proud of my first perm. I used to love to pull and release the springy curls, until an older girl at school noticed and mocked me. At that moment I realized that how you feel about your hair should be a private matter, only shared with those in close confidence.

My hair was powerful; it could change my mood or ruin my day in an instant. Yet I would gladly take any bad hair day over *this*. I had always shed a lot of hair on a daily basis, so I didn't notice anything unusual until the hair stylist clued me in one day. Nothing prepared me for the shock of a seeing a quarter-sized patch of scalp exposed on the side of my head. My hair was falling out, and I was only nineteen years old.

I scheduled an appointment with my family doctor. After filling out the paperwork and being weighed and looked over, I was eager for an explanation and a prescription. The doctor looked baffled. "I need to ask you a question: have you been pulling out your hair?"

The first time he asked, I was incredulous. Not only did this man not provide any helpful information, but he had the nerve to blame me for my predicament? I fumed inwardly.

"One more time, are you sure you haven't been pulling out your hair?" The second time he asked I felt a brief flash of pity for him, as his helplessness reflected my own. The almighty doctor confessed, "I'm stumped."

He sent me to a dermatologist, a kinder, gentler man with a superior bedside manner. But rather than cheering me up, his upbeat demeanor only emphasized the gloom I felt. Alopecia areata. My condition had a name, but no definitive cause or cure. "Your immune system is attacking the hair follicles, causing hair loss. Alopecia areata is an unpredictable disease. Sometimes it goes into remission, but it may come back again later." What was the point in naming the stupid thing if it didn't change anything? I left the dermatologist's office angry and frustrated.

My horror turned to shame as the bald spots began to multiply. Each morning I dreaded looking in the mirror. After my shower, I would brush my hair carefully so as to not disturb the fragile strands. The stark contrast of the pale, smooth skin amidst my dark brown hair made it hard to hide the bald patches. I painstakingly arranged my hair with bobby pins and hairspray and prayed for no rain or wind as I left the house.

I tried reasoning with myself. Hair was just a trivial, vain attachment. However, I was nineteen. My self-image was entwined with my physical appearance, and my attractiveness was wrapped up in my hair. With each chunk of hair I lost, I felt diminished and demoralized.

Months passed. Nothing was working, and I was hopeless. Many bald spots were scattered all over my head. Hats were no longer an accessory but a necessity. Daily application of Minoxidil and frequent steroid injections from the dermatologist showed no visible effect. "It's only a matter of time," the doctor told me. "We don't know for sure what causes it, but in most cases, the hair grows back. Just be patient."

Despite all the treatments, the only thing growing was my depression. The hair loss seemed to spread with my negativity, yet I felt powerless against my despair. As more time passed, even my doctor's voice sounded less hopeful. "Yours is a very unusual case. It's rare to see such extensive hair loss, but it could grow back any day. The body is a perplexing organism." His smile appeared shakier. My fate felt sealed by the sadness in his eyes.

This doctor knew my whole story—the assault that preceded the alopecia, the fracture to my eye, my unwillingness to talk about it. My thick, impenetrable wall of sadness blocked out even my family and friends. I rejected their sympathetic gestures. They couldn't understand what I was going through, and I didn't want to talk about my feelings. I just wanted a solution. I didn't see the connection yet.

In the midst of it all, I went on with my daily life of classes, work, and even going out. I preferred the busyness, the distractions. One night while out at a club called The Garage, I met a guy. Just like in the movies, our eyes connected from across the room. I was drawn to the hint of mischief in his eyes and walked over to meet him. I felt instantly at ease around him, and I almost laughed when he introduced himself. His name, Fred, seemed to suit a grandfather better than this animated, childlike man.

From that point on, my days were largely spent with Fred. His goofy playfulness magically eased my burden. Fred's nonchalant acceptance of my hair condition combined with his own lack of self-consciousness granted me true inner freedom. In his presence, my laughter flowed easily, and with it, optimism reappeared.

Months later, fine baby fuzz began to appear on my scalp. And over the course of the next year, my hair slowly grew back. It took much longer for me to understand fully what had caused my condition.

Sometimes I think back to that nineteen-year-old girl. I remember her frustration with a body that seemed to turn on her, to punish her for events outside of her control. In the many years since, I've done a lot of inner work and meditation. No longer afraid to face my feelings, I have new tools to employ when life unexpectedly gets crazy.

Alopecia has subsequently returned twice during stressful times in my life. In each instance, I've stayed calm and taken time to nurture myself and find joy in my daily life. No more steroids, no more treatments. The single bald patch didn't spread either time. The hair grew back naturally.

Now, as a hypnotherapist, I understand that emotions affect the physical body. I feel blessed to be able to help others who struggle with alopecia. My experience enabled me to assist people struggling not only with alopecia, but with any mind-body affliction. There are so many.

Ultimately, it was love and acceptance that made my hair grow. Love makes everything grow. I don't believe that Fred showed up in my life by chance. Through his love, I learned to see myself in a new way: not with my eyes, but with my heart.

Transforming Darkness into Sunshine

GLORIA PIANTEK

Golden ribbons of light flickered through the blinds, spreading across the top of my dad's silver hair as he stared down at the living room rug. He was so strong, so compassionate, so loving. His actions taught me the importance of helping others and making them feel confident and valued. I asked him once how he learned to care so much, and he just smiled and said, "I felt the pain of failing, and no one needs that in their life."

Now, as his heart grew weaker, he couldn't breathe as easily anymore. His legs swelled to double in size, making walking a challenge. Gone was the vibrant man who ran beside me as I tried to ride my bicycle, and patiently put worms on my hook so I could discover how much fun it was to fish.

Most times Mom was at his side, but today she'd asked me to stay with him while she shopped for some groceries. We shared this quiet moment together, interrupted only when he looked up and with a labored breath said, "Gloria, I'm not afraid to die, but I want you to remember something. We gather strength from those who come before us. Promise me that you'll never stop trying to make this a better world."

"Dad, don't even talk about leaving us," I quickly responded as I knelt next to his rocking chair. "You're going to be fine. Mom always knows how to nurse everyone back to health." I lifted my face, attempting to hide my tear-filled eyes and sniffling nose.

He gently placed his hand under my right ear, guided his fingers around my face to my other ear while saying, "Remember this: I am always going to be with you. You will never be alone."

My dad passed soon after, and although he never saw me achieve my dreams, he was always in my heart.

As fate would have it, I became a teacher and found myself working in the field of special education and reading remediation. How intriguing that my spiritual path led me right into the lives of children who were experiencing failure and a world full of challenging problems, just as my dad did.

The students who failed state-mandated tests, day-dreamed, worked too quickly, wouldn't complete their assignments, or lacked basic academic skills were all sent to me. I quickly realized they were talented in many areas, but they didn't view themselves as successful. For them, school meant a place for failing. In fact, one boy even proudly said, "Hey, I never passed English. Not even one time." It was like a badge of honor for him, but it pained me to hear it.

Each day I was exposed to the hopelessness that these students carried around like baggage. I heard them say, "Why doesn't the state give me enough time on the tests to show them what I really know?" "I like being with you, but I just hate being in this dumb class." "I can't do this—I just can't do this." Their comments resonated with me as I recalled my own feelings when I struggled to learn new academic skills. I understood their pain but felt powerless to help them solve their problems.

I welcomed the weekends, since they provided me with a respite from the negativity of the classroom, and I plunged into fun baking and cake decorating projects. One afternoon, as I mounted a cluster of rings over the top of a cream-colored anniversary cake for my best friend, I remembered when my high school teacher gave me a poor grade in art. I accepted his opinion as fact and believed that I couldn't do anything involving artistic expression. The power of his words and actions made me feel like a failure in that subject, and my thoughts and emotions reflected his criticism for years afterward. That failing attitude prevailed until my mother casually commented on how artistic my cakes were. It took me twenty years before I viewed myself as having any artistic talent. At that point, something inside me clicked: grades and teachers create attitudes of success or failure, and my evaluations could change students' lives.

That night, as I closed my eyes and drifted off to sleep, I saw a bright white light appear which made me feel warm and peaceful. Heavenly puffs of clouds floated into view, and I saw my father wearing his large silver cross around his neck. He looked directly at me and said only two words: "Remember Earth." I woke up wondering what this dream meant. Could this be something my father wanted me to do? I repeated the word, "Earth."

Then, like rays of sunshine streaming through the windows, I knew the answer. My father's name was Edward Arthur Rudolph Theodore Holz—E.A.R.T.H.—and he wanted me to remember our last conversation when he said, "I felt the pain of failing, and no one needs that in their life."

I recalled how he used to sit outside on the porch steps talking to the neighborhood boys, encouraging them to embrace their talents and always ask questions. He believed the love of learning grows from one's roots and is inside all of us. Yes, he wanted me to help my students see themselves as academic winners.

"Please God, help me change the lives of my students and eliminate this cycle of failing, replacing it with a feeling of success," I prayed.

On Monday morning I walked into my classroom carrying my father's words, a renewed sense of purpose, and a personal challenge. I couldn't change the state-mandated rules, remedial curriculums, or attendance requirements, but I could try to help my students develop ownership over learning the material I was teaching. I decided to change my evaluation procedures, which gave them an opportunity to earn points for completing assignments and mastering new reading and writing skills. Modifying the grading procedures offered them a way to control the grade they received on their report card. It took some time, but this opened the first door of change.

You can imagine my delight when I saw my students counting their skill points and smiling. They were becoming engaged in their learning process, generating a positive commitment rather than a "give-up" attitude. Visually having some immediate external rewards transferred to internal motivation and helped them to view learning as a road to success rather than a dead end. They were transforming.

Having my father share his painful experiences allowed me to open a door of opportunity for many other students who would now see sunshine in education rather than darkness. As I reflected on this optimistic direction, I couldn't help but wonder if these ideas would stay with them when they left my class and the road of life was rough.

I am so grateful I had the opportunity to see how this approach could change their lives. One day, a young boy named Marcus approached my desk and said, "We gotta leave the country and can't return. Please give me some reading homework? I'll do 'em and send 'em to you to check. Can ya do that for me?"

"Of course I'll do it," I said, gathering up the reading materials for him. As he left the room, I understood how difficult his situation was, and I admired his determination.

Six months later, I walked into the mailroom and saw a large brown envelope near my teacher's box. As I opened it, I couldn't believe what was inside. Tears filled my eyes as I stared at the printed answers on those completed papers. Tucked inside the pages was a beautiful thank-you letter asking me to grade the papers and send them back so he could correct any errors. Yes, inside of him was that everlasting drive to succeed.

Holding those papers in my hands, I knew Dad was right. What everyone calls failure is an opportunity to grow. It was clear that a person's positive mind-set is the source of energy for igniting a powerful fail-safe spirit. My job is to remember that for myself, and to help facilitate that transformation in others. One just needs to look up with optimism and passion instead of staring down at the street in lifelong failure. It's really true, there are no mistakes, only opportunities to learn and make your dreams come true.

Envisioning a Life of Health and Well-Being

ROBYN BENSON, DOM

When my patients ask me how I first became interested in health care and Chinese medicine, I often share with them this quote from Mark Twain: "The two most important days in your life are the day you are born and the day you find out why."

My "why" began to take shape when I was just five years old. My youngest brother, David Alden, was born with a hole in his heart and suffered from brain damage. My parents were dedicated to keeping our little brother alive despite the prognosis, so we would drive six hours each way to the best pediatric cardiologist in New York City.

At six months of age, little David finally succumbed to his damaged heart and passed away. As my mother, father, older brother, and grandparents walked out the front door to go to his funeral I remember feeling that was the worst day of my life. I wondered about life and death, and I questioned why we had to experience such suffering. It broke my hear to think about what my baby brother had had to endure. More than anything, I wanted to be the doctor who could have saved my brother's life.

My conviction stayed with me, and when I was in fifth grade I chose to spend Career Day shadowing Dr. Reinsfield. In the morning Dr. Reinsfield took me to two nursing homes. As we entered the lobby of the first nursing home, I was anxious and immediately turned to walk back out the front door. Dr. Reinsfield gently took my hand and said, "Robyn, I want to introduce you to my friends," and I reluctantly turned around and accompanied him. The smell of stale food, mold, and urine was overwhelming. People were talking in languages I'd never heard before. All I could think about was how these people had ended up here, and, more importantly, what could have been done to prevent them from becoming ill in the first place. Dr. Reinsfield patiently answered my questions. He told me that old age and poor lifestyle choices were the main reasons most people ended up in nursing homes. The strange languages, he explained, were a result of dementia and Alzheimer's, both diseases of the aging body and mind.

"Oh my God," I thought. "I do not want to die in a place like this; and I don't want others to die the way my brother did, alone in a hospital room." That night I went home and declared to my family, "I know what I'm doing for a career. I am going to dedicate my life to helping all my friends, family, and loved ones to live well and to stay well." From that point on, I committed myself to learning everything I could about medicine and wellness.

At the age of fifteen, my conviction would be renewed when I faced another tragedy. My dear friend Todd was diagnosed with leukemia. We ran cross-country together and were science partners. Todd started chemo and radiation, and he got so skinny, but he still kept on running with me. One day he said to me, "You know what, Robyn, I just want to live long enough to run a marathon."

Sadly, Todd never had the chance to run that marathon. He died on April 20, 1980. Exactly a year later, my friend Tim and I ran the Boston Marathon in honor of Todd and his dream. We were still far too young to run officially, but we were determined to do this for Todd. I met many dedicated people along that twenty-six mile journey from Hopkinton, Massachusetts, to Boston. Many had healed from a terminal disease, or they were running for their daughter, or their grandmother, or other loved ones. Seeing people in wheelchairs was such an inspiration. As I crossed the finish line that day, I rededicated my life's work to health, wellness, and living my life to the fullest each day. Todd's life had ended early, but his spirit would live inside me for the rest of my life.

I went on to study sports medicine at the University of Virginia and then complete a four-year program in acupuncture and Chinese medicine. For thirteen years, I happily ran a successful alternative medicine private practice.

But eventually I could no longer suppress the recurring vision I had of starting a comprehensive, holistic health care center—one which would have many practitioners and offer a variety of options for healing. At the same time I was at a crossroads career-wise; I was feeling the effects of burnout. I was becoming numb to the problems I was hearing daily, and I would lie down to sleep at night haunted by the cries of despair on my tables.

Then one snowy New Mexico Sunday, I stood on the bare piece of land that would one day become Santa Fe Soul Health and Healing. I was overcome by an exhilarating sense of rightness, and although I was a little frightened I could almost see this vibrant, inclusive, cutting-edge center I imagined sprouting from the ground before my eyes.

During the next eighteen months, as I let spiritual wisdom take the lead, I witnessed incredible, life-altering healing in myself and several practitioners who joined me in planning and building the center. The vision I had carried with me for two decades was finally taking shape. Finally on May 23, 2005, Santa Fe Soul Health and Healing Center opened with twenty-five talented independent practitioners offering forty different healing services.

Today, thousands of people have come through our doors to experience deep healing, Deeksha, Puja, dance, yoga, and other life-enhancing workshops in our state-of-the-art movement room. Patients and practitioners alike have experienced a shift in consciousness, subsidence of ailments, and peace in their hearts, and I am in awe of what we have accomplished.

This is what co-creation is all about; this is what surrendering to those persistent voices brings to life.

I knew loss intimately from an early age, but I also knew happiness. And over time I came to understand that events do not happen *to us* in many cases, but rather *for us* to learn, grow, and step into our passion, potential, and purpose. From sorrow and tragedy come growth and transformation, and through these hardships I learned the important of living well, aging beautifully, and loving fully. Make no mistake, these early experiences—visiting a nursing home on Career Day, and grieving the loss of my little brother and my friend Todd—motivated me to accomplish far more in my twenty-year medical career than I believe I would have been capable of doing otherwise. I don't know how my entire life's work could help but be altered by these life-changing experiences.

I believe that love is a bond more powerful than death, and I still carry my love for David and Todd with me every day. If I can leave you with just one thing, let it be this: your health is your true wealth. Self-care (of the mind, body, *and* spirit) is a way of life, not an event, and we have the power to make choices each and every day that will bring about health and happiness. Make the most of them.

The Gifts of the Angels

SIOBHAN COULTER

"These babies are starving! Look at how much weight they've lost already. And they're sleeping too long. They are starting to become dehydrated and jaundiced, and they will die if you don't do something about it!" Only fifty-six hours into motherhood, and a midwife was berating me as I struggled to breast-feed my newborn twins.

"I'm doing my best, but my milk hasn't come in yet." Knowing babies sometimes reject the breast after being given the bottle, I explained, "My husband and I want our sons to be breast-fed so we don't want to give them formula if we don't have to. But what other options are there?"

"Nothing that you believe in," the midwife said.

Well, that wasn't helping anyone, on any level, I thought—but I was about to be proved wrong.

The words spoken by this midwife angel (as I came to think of her) started a chain of events that I never would have anticipated and will be forever grateful for. Her opinions, rudely spoken and harshly delivered though they were, were undeniably grounded in truth. I had to admit she was right. My babies *were* hungry, and they needed food soon.

We gave my sons purified water to prevent dehydration, but it was a poor substitute for the food they desperately needed, and their cries were letting everyone in the maternity ward know. My husband and I were terrified. We were in a country town more than an hour from our home, in a hospital that accommodated our wish to give birth naturally.

Catapulted into action, my guardian angels set about doing everything they could to help. My Dad drove nine hours that day, searching far and wide for anything that could help, while my Mum checked into a local motel so that she would be available to stay with us at the hospital until we were all allowed to go home.

Close friends called my natural practitioners for advice on supplements and remedies that could increase my milk production and then collected the prescribed treatments, while others tended to the boys. Miraculously, every practitioner they contacted answered their phone (despite being closed on Sundays), and every item they shopped for they found. I, meanwhile, busied myself making best friends with the double breast pump and tried to rest in between the boys' twice-hourly feeds.

That night another angel appeared, a midwife named

Vicki. We first met Vicki the morning after the boys were born, and I felt instantly connected to her. When she walked into our room that evening I burst into tears. "Can you believe it? Someone didn't turn up for their shift, so they called me!" she said. Vicki was a popular home-birth midwife, and she usually only worked at the hospital two shifts a week. I couldn't believe our luck.

I told Vicki about my sons' state, and she immediately thought of another new mother, Phillipa. Seven weeks earlier, Vicki had helped Phillipa give birth to a premature baby boy, and he had been in the ICU since his birth. Unable to stay with him, Phillipa had returned home. Yet she remained committed to breast-feeding her baby. Every day, she delivered pumped breast milk to the hospital for her son. What wasn't consumed was frozen as an emergency store for him.

Phillipa's son was scheduled to be released from the hospital the next day, and she was staying with him on the maternity ward that evening. Phillipa heard my sons' cries down the hall and, like any connected mother, intuitively knew that my boys needed milk. Without even being asked, she immediately offered us her frozen breast milk. We discussed the possible health concerns of donor milk and decided to accept Phillipa's gift. After nearly seventy-two hours of life, my boys finally had their first real meal, and that night we all slept peacefully for several hours.

In the days that followed, I got only snippets of sleep as I cared for my new sons. During one of those naps I had an amazing dream that has profoundly changed how I see the world. In this dream, I saw my life from a universal perspective. Every part of my life up to that point was set out before me—every person I'd ever met, every major event I'd experienced, all the lessons I'd learned, all the unexpected bends and turns I'd experienced—and I saw now how every single aspect was interconnected. I was in awe of the complexity and detail of what I was seeing, yet I felt incredibly calm with this immense expansion of my awareness. I knew that no matter what happened from now on, everything was ultimately as it should be; it was perfect.

Then my dream began to shift. It was like zooming in from a satellite view to street view. I now saw my life as a linear timeline. I was stunned by the seemingly easy flow of my life, given the complex orchestration occurring behind the scenes.

Then my dream changed again. Like the pages in a pop-up book, the next page began to open, causing my timeline perspective to fold down, and my new universal awareness began to fade. The next page was glowing white, as if a star were shining out from the book itself. It was beautiful, and I felt pure wonder and gratitude. At this point I was given two pieces of knowledge: First, I had just passed an important milestone; the first part of my life was now over, and a new chapter was beginning. Second, I had the tools I needed for the second part of my life; all I had to do was use them. What a wonderful gift.

I awoke with a new clarity I'd never experienced before. I wasn't shown how my future would play out, thank goodness—that would probably spoil all the fun! But I do know that as my life unfolds I don't have to worry about the hows and the whys, because that is being handled by something far greater than my conscious mind. We are always being supported and loved by the universe. We just have to trust.

Several years have passed since that night at the hospital, but Phillipa's gift will forever be in my heart, and every night my angels are in my prayers. We have stayed in touch with Phillipa and Vicki, and we learned that Phillipa and my husband attended the same university, are in the same line of work, and on at least two occasions that we know of they almost worked at the same company. Obviously, our meeting was fated, but I am grateful that our paths crossed when we needed her most.

Every time I look at my beautiful, energetic boys I am reminded of Phillipa's pure-hearted gift of love, and the knowledge that I gained from that time. Everyone and everything is connected, and we are all connected for a divine reason. Every day I try to recognize and thank the angels who cross my path—obvious angels, like Phillipa and Vicki, and more behind-the-scenes angels, like the first midwife whom I didn't recognize as being a helpful and loving angel at the time, but to whom I will always be grateful.

Finally, I am grateful for the divine guidance of my dream. When I remember not to worry I give myself the freedom to *live* with love and peace, and, best of all, to *enjoy* the ups and downs of my life. Knowing that the universe provides and that over time it will become apparent that things are as they should be has been such a gift as I navigate this second part of my life with my husband and sons.

Heartache Is the Greatest Gift

Susana M. Silverhøj

On the 28th of January 2009 I got pregnant. What a joy. When I took the pregnancy test a few weeks later I couldn't believe it—such love was floating through me. I was sitting on the bathroom floor, watching a blue line on a stick, and I fell totally and unconditionally in love with this little embryo. I loved her just as much as my other two children. I was ecstatic. I cried out of gratefulness and happiness.

Three weeks later I started to have stomach cramps, and I called the doctor for a checkup. I had never been nervous during my other pregnancies, but now I could feel that there was something wrong. The doctor sent me to the hospital for a scan. The scan showed that the baby wasn't as big as she should be at that point in the pregnancy, but that could mean that she was conceived later than I thought, so I was

61

told not to worry. It only meant that the baby was too small to be able to see any heartbeat. I had to take a blood test and then return a week later.

That was one of the worst weeks of my life. I was thrown back and forth between hope and despair. I cried and kept on thinking, "My baby is dead." Other moments I felt faith that she was OK, that it was just my mind playing a trick on me.

Then D-day came. The day when we would finally get the results—was the baby alive or not?

Then, the bomb. The bad news. We had lost our baby. All hope was lost. I had to have an abortion since the baby's heart never started to beat. She only reached the age of five weeks and six days.

When we walked into the blue and cold hospital room where the abortion would take place, everything felt surreal. I felt like I was in a movie, and I could almost see myself from the outside. My heart was broken. Large, warm tears were pouring down my cheeks and it felt like I was about to die. The words "I lost my baby, my baby is dead, she is gone" were pounding in my head. I could hardly breathe. My chest cramped from the pain.

My husband and I hung on to each other tight so as to not fall apart completely. We were crying like we had never cried before. Normally my husband is the strong one, holding me up, helping me, and allowing me to cry like a baby. The beautiful thing at this moment was that we were crying together, supporting each other at the same time. It was such a peaceful moment. We were one in this moment of

No Mistakes

chaos and pain. Our hearts were bleeding, but our love was so strong—for each other, and for our children.

He was by my side all day while I had all the drugs and pills, waiting for the bleeding to start. The nurses were sweet and had such empathy. I felt the support I needed from all around.

We got to go home late in the afternoon when the bleeding started. After an hour at home I had to go to the bathroom. When I sat down, all this warm, thick blood came pouring out like a flood. And then I felt a big lump coming out of me.

I flushed my baby out in the toilet. It was one of the most heartbreaking moments of my life. I felt horribly guilty. I was disgusted with myself. What kind of parent was I? I wanted to pick my baby up and hold her in my arms forever. I didn't want to let her go.

That night my husband and I lay in each other's arms and talked. I wanted to say that this was the worst day of my life, but I couldn't. Despite the awful experience of losing a child, no matter how small she was, it was a beautiful day full of love. My husband and I were closer than ever before, we felt compassion from the people around us, and we felt the deep, all-encompassing love for our children. So it was a strange day, heartbreaking and yet full of love. Painful, but compassionate.

There have been times since the miscarriage when I have wondered if I did something wrong, if I could have done something differently. What if it was my fault I had lost her?

What if I had listened to my body sooner, or didn't stress as much, or . . .

The grief and pain lasted for years. I still cry once in a while, and I can still feel my love for her. But I can also see the magic and gifts of the experience. I have learned that you can never measure another person's pain. A miscarriage early in the pregnancy might not create much pain for some, but it could be torture for others. People tried to help me by saying things like "It was something that wasn't right;" "At least it wasn't a real baby yet;" or "It would be worse if you lost the baby after it was born." Well, those comments didn't help, because from the moment that baby was made I loved her just as much as my other two children who survived. I had named her Alma (which means "spirit" in Spanish).

The week before the doctors told me I had lost her, I prayed every day. I prayed for Alma to stay with me, to give me the greatest gift I *thought* she could ever give me—to let me hold her in my arms and love and take care of her forever. But I know that her gift was to help me to open my heart and to stay vulnerable. I have had great sufferings in my life before, experiences such as sexual abuse, dealing with alcoholic family members, and having an unfaithful first love when I was a teen, which made me close my heart. It was hard for me to let anyone in. Every time I felt vulnerable I shut down again and again, leaving me with a lot of suffering and pain. Alma helped me crack my heart wide open with no return. She gave me the gift of living from my heart, cracking the wall I had built around it and teaching me to reconnect with myself.

Children are the best gift in so many ways. Children are our best teachers. They mirror you, they give you unconditional love, and something higher than yourself to live for. We were blessed with a healthy baby boy after this experience, and because of the loss of Alma I have been so grateful and enjoy my wonderful children even more. I don't take them for granted. I appreciate them, and life, even more. I live more. I love more.

The spirit of Alma was also a gift designed so I could have the experience of losing someone I love. Now I can help others with this experience and feel more empathy. I know that this experience was for the higher good even though I felt so much pain throughout the process. Or maybe it's that the more pain, and the more suffering there is, the greater the gift. It never feels like it in the moment, but looking back, experiences like these have proven to be amazing blessings.

On Easter 2009 I received a "message" from Alma. I heard this voice in my head saying: "Mom, if your love was enough, I would have stayed."

I knew it was her, and a lot of the guilt I had been carrying with me disappeared after that day. I understood this wasn't about me not loving her enough, or her not loving me—her death happened for the higher good.

I will always remember and love Alma, and I feel grateful for the experience. Love is more than life—love is everything in and beyond time and space. There is a higher purpose to everything, we just have to stay open for the gifts we receive. They come in all shapes. Even death.

Starting Over

Having a Second Chance to "Get It Right"

CAROL J. CRAIG

From a very young age I was known as the kid who knew no strangers. I was gregarious and made friends easily, and this served me well through adolescence and on into adulthood.

I also found myself in trouble a lot, though. I was a bright student, but I remember being constantly bored or unchallenged in American public school. I would finish my work quickly and then create problems with others who were still working. I got a lot of negative attention at school and then again at home, where I would be punished for whatever mischief I had gotten into. And so it went through my entire educational experience.

When I was in middle school, I found something that made the world seem a bit more exciting. I found alcohol.

Surprisingly, I could drink and none of the adults around me suspected a thing. I think they all thought I was just a spirited, outgoing girl. By the time I got into high school, in 1974, I was a full-fledged alcoholic and no one had any idea, including me. I thought I was just a recreational drinker. During this time kids were experimenting with drugs, alcohol, sex, and rock 'n' roll. I was starting high school right in the heart of the era, and I was quite functional in the role of free-spirited teenager. I worked a part-time job throughout high school and even managed to graduate early.

I went on to study forestry management and earned a bachelor of science degree from Southern Illinois University Carbondale. According to society's measure of success, I was right on track. What was not being measured, however, was the fact that I was pretty much drinking and partying seven days a week. I appeared to be functioning well, so nobody was concerned about my social habits, and I hung out with friends who exhibited the same behaviors, so it all seemed acceptable and normal.

I'd done an internship in Colorado for the United States Forest Service while I was still in college, and I was able to acquire a full-time position there after graduation. I headed to the tourist area of Summit County to begin my life as a "grown-up." I brought my old habits along with me, only now life wasn't broken up into semesters; life continued seamlessly year after year, without winter vacation or spring break. I had a lot of issues with my drinking, but I blamed other people, places, and things for my troubles and didn't really make the connection between my difficulties with alcohol and the fact that my life was becoming unmanageable.

After four and a half years of living at the level of basic survival, I decided to move to Phoenix to start over once again. I had a sister there whom I stayed with until I found a place. I got a job as the manager of a twenty-four-hour store, so I had little time to be bored, and I was making good money. I spent most of my free time with my sister and her kids exploring Phoenix, and I was managing my drinking habit by avoiding the bar scene.

After about a year, I was offered an opportunity to move to Prescott, Arizona. While others may enjoy putting down roots and living in one spot for a lifetime, I am a person with wings, who likes to fly often. I've never been very good at sitting still for long, and I jumped at the chance for a change.

Once I transferred up north I needed to find new buddies to hang with. My first night in town I didn't have electricity hooked up yet, so shortly after the sun went down I found myself feeling antsy and decided to go out. I went to the Bird Cage Saloon on Whiskey Row, a famous block of bars in Prescott. It had been a while since I had been in a bar, but it felt *very* familiar, and before I knew it I was back into my old ways. I became fast friends with many of the bar owners in town and quickly found myself in the center of a remarkable group of people who all liked to party and carry on just like I did—and they all appeared to be quite functional. I treasured my newfound comrades, and we had fantastic excursions regularly to Las Vegas, Laughlin, and Lake Pleasant.

Five years slipped by. I was now a well-established member of the Prescott community; I had built a house and had settled down. I didn't want to change a thing. What I didn't realize at the time was that I was back into my alcoholic lifestyle worse than ever. I was in complete denial of what a train wreck my life had become.

And then I was in a car accident that changed my life. Fortunately, no one was seriously hurt. But I got a DUI, and everything that comes with it: fines, court costs, drinking classes, community service, and counseling. At the time I didn't realize how this mistake could possibly turn out well. I really thought it was the worst thing that could ever happen. It wasn't until years later that I realized that car accident gave me a second chance at living.

During a court-mandated counseling session, I shared my twenty-three-year partying history with a complete stranger who made me feel safe. I was floating when I left. I'd had an epiphany. I was being given a chance to get my act together before I killed myself, or, worse yet, someone else. Right then and there, I made a life-changing decision to sober up and create a new life for myself. It was the first time I had even acknowledged that I had a problem.

I sold my house, moved across the country to my mother's home in Rhode Island, and began "drying out." I joined a local 12-step group, where I attended ninety meetings in ninety weeks instead of the recommended ninety days. Yes, I was stubborn. It was not an easy road, but I am proud to report that I have just entered my twenty-first year sober.

Over the past twenty-odd years, I have accomplished many amazing things. I studied environmental engineering at the University of Rhode Island and then went on to earn my master's in education.

About two years into my sobriety I joined the Unitarian Universalist community, and that experience has enlightened my life. About twelve years ago, I joined the Clear Heart Buddhist sangha, and that has also had a profound effect on my outlook on life. I am eternally grateful to the lovely, caring people I have met through both of these organizations.

I taught abroad for seven years in Trinidad and Tobago; Cairo, Egypt; and Nairobi, Kenya. At age forty-eight, I married for the first time. I met my husband in Trinidad and Tobago, and we travel the world together creating a fantastic life. Last year I took a sabbatical and wrote a book about our love story, one that never would have been possible had I not volunteered in Kenya the summers of 2005–08. It was while volunteering there that I learned the secret to happiness from people who live in extreme poverty. This experience allowed me to look past the material things I used to judge someone's worth by, and I became a minimalist. My husband and I don't have a single demographic trait in common, but we are happily married and living in Trinidad.

I'm sorry that it took a potentially life-threatening car accident to propel me onto my path of recovery, but life often forces us into uncomfortable circumstances. Through them, we experience the growth necessary to complete our individual destinies. These pushes often feel like shoves, and life can manifest some strange ways to get us to pay attention. But when we recognize these challenges as such we can reap great rewards.

I do consider that car accident to be a true miracle. It put me on a different path, one that has given me a new, wider perspective on life. I have hope now, and I believe in the capacity of anyone to change and to make the life that he or she was meant to live.

Love Down Under

CAROLE J TOMS ND

Some of the most challenging times in life can also turn out to be the most amazing opportunities. That has been my experience. We are given challenges to allow us to grow on our path to awareness, and we are also given opportunities to let others help us along the way.

Our ego says, loud and clear, "Go this way," and we race to follow. Then our greater consciousness speaks up. "For your greater good you need to go in this direction," it says. But what if we do not want to listen? This is when hardship ensues. After years of practice, I have learned to listen to the soft voice of greater consciousness rather than the booming voice of my ego, and it has shown me my true path.

Let me tell you my story.

I am originally from Victoria, in the southeast of Australia. After eighteen years of working as a nurse and in community services management, I moved up north to Queensland to attend graduate school in naturopathy and homeopathy. I had found the natural alternatives to be a better way to go. I was a mature age student, and I loved it. Near the end of my fourth year I was wrapping up my final exams and thinking about what would come next. I wanted to remain in Queensland and establish my clinic there.

With our exams out of the way, everyone celebrated. Graduation was imminent, and we were all having fun. I felt the excitement too, but I was suffering from acute back pain at the time. The pain was excruciating and I needed help. But being so focused on my studies, I was not tuned in to Spirit, so I decided to ask my dreams for relief. My dreams have always given me answers when I am not listening to the quiet voice of Spirit.

Before going to sleep one night, I asked what I needed to do to relieve my back pain. "Please tell me what I am doing wrong. Whatever it is, I will change it," I promised. That night I had a series of three dreams, and one by one they unfolded my future life plan. My first dream told me to leave the north; my second dream told me to head south; and my final dream told me to go back to my home state in the far south. I was reluctant to move back to my home, but I knew deep down that these dreams had come from my higher consciousness, so I agreed to follow this path.

When I awoke the next morning I had no pain—none

whatsoever. Not only that, but I jumped out of bed like an energetic ten-year-old. Part of me was much happier in the north, and I viewed going back to my old home state as regressing to a past I had left behind. But I had promised myself I would follow my spirit, so I made the arrangements to move after graduation.

I arrived back home to learn that both of my parents were in need of my help. I bought a house in the country and started setting up my naturopathic and homeopathic clinic. I lived about forty-five minutes west of the city, and I would drive to the city each day for work. After work, at least twice a week, I would visit my parents on the eastern side of the city an hour's drive farther away.

My new business had massive start-up costs, and money was extremely tight. I was filling my gas tank every day, and I had to start skipping meals to make ends meet. I could not afford the cost of heating, so I would quickly eat my dinner, shower, and then jump into bed for warmth. Life was tight, really tight. I eventually found myself unable to cope and spent a week sick in bed. There was no food in the house, and I was miles away from anyone I knew. The local shops would not deliver, so I reluctantly asked a neighbor to pick up a takeout meal for me. I coped on my own after that, eating the equivalent of one meal a day.

Through all this hardship I knew I had made the right decision to return home. Without me close by, my parents would have been in a far worse state, and I would have always regretted not being there when they needed me if I'd stayed far away. When I was younger they were always there for me, and I valued that greatly.

My father died a few months after I arrived, and I was thankful I had been able to spend some valuable time with him before his passing. In the weeks leading up to his death he had several dreams that warned him of his impending transformation and journey to the other side. I suggested that he do exactly what he wanted to do, complete what he wanted to complete, and see who he wanted to see while he still had the time. He did that, and when the time came he was ready to pass over with no regrets.

I then turned my attention to my mother, who also needed my help. She was frail and on oxygen 24/7. We were able to get help for her during the week, but on the weekends I had to take over. I would arrive in the morning with breakfast and then get her showered and dressed. I made her lunch, put tea in a heated container, and made sure she was comfortable. I would then leave and return at 5:00 p.m. to get her dinner. When she was ready I helped her into her nightgown and into bed. I would make her hot chocolate and leave for the night, and then return the next day to do it all over again. Occasionally I rang my sister, who also lived in the country, and asked her to come because I needed a break. She would stay for two weekends and then I would take over again.

It was a year before we could get Mom into a convalescent home. When she moved in I was free on the weekends for the first time in over a year. I visited regularly, and we would often take walks together; she on her mobility scooter, while

I walked alongside. I have fond memories of those walks. Mom eventually passed three years after my father.

A couple of weeks before my father died I met my current husband. I had been married and divorced once before, and my second husband could not have been more different from my first. They were like chalk and cheese. Greg was gentle, kind, and helpful. When we got married my mother could not attend, so I called her and she listened to the service and the speeches by phone. My two grown-up daughters were my attendants, and we all had a wonderful day. If I had stayed up north I never would have met my soul mate.

Six years ago Greg had the opportunity to leave his job and begin contracting. After a few contracts he was offered a job in Queensland. As that contract kept being extended for longer and longer periods of time, we decided to sell our house and move permanently to the north. I finally returned to where my heart belonged. Greg and I have now been married for fifteen happy years, and for the last five we have lived in the northern state I loved and left long ago.

Everything really does happen for a reason. I followed my inner voice and did what the greater consciousness wanted me to do for the good of others and myself. I knew intuitively that I needed to return home to care for my aging parents and to meet my soul mate. The path my life took from then on opened before me. I am so grateful to have had the opportunity to help my parents the way they helped me, and I am grateful to have found Greg. He had waited all his life to meet me and had never married. Greg was there in my greatest time of need. When I was starving he fed me; when my parents passed to the other side he nourished me with tender love. If I had done what my ego wanted and stayed in the north, I would have moved away from my greater awareness, away from what my soul needed to experience. Following my ego would have meant not being available to help my parents when they needed me most, and I would have regretted that choice for the rest of my life. And it would have meant never meeting Greg. I would have satisfied my ego, but at what price? So you see . . . everything happens for a reason.

What Time Is It?

KYLE WEAVER AND SCOTT EDMUND MILLER

I was fourteen years old on the day that my identity was erased.

I opened my eyes and found myself lying on a cot. A tubular fluorescent light flickered directly above me, casting a field of shadows that danced across the perforated ceiling tiles.

I shifted my gaze to a man who was seated by my side. "Coach" was printed across the breast of his T-shirt. It seemed like a strange name for a man, but no stranger than the dance of light above him. He was staring at me, and were it not for the kindness and concern in his eyes, I might have found the whole situation a bit creepy.

There was a burning question on my mind. It was the only thing I could think to say. "What time is it?" I asked.

The man winced as if the question had somehow wounded

him. He reached out and rubbed my shoulder, and then he said, "It's still 2:03, Scott."

I wasn't sure who "Scott" was. Just the same, Coach's manner seemed to set me at ease, and I promptly blacked out.

When I came to, I was lying on a cot and "Coach" was seated beside me. I could hear a couple boys somewhere across the room making quite a fuss.

"Is he gonna be OK?" one of them asked pleadingly.

"We heard his head crack against the volleyball court from all the way across the field," said another.

There was a strange, burning question on my mind. I didn't understand why it felt so important. "What time is it?" I asked.

||||||

It turns out that amnesia doesn't always play out the way it's portrayed in the movies or on TV. In my experience, my memory was being continually wiped clean. Every few minutes or so, my mind kept rebooting like a faulty computer hard drive desperately trying to reengage. Its only line of code was: *What time is it?*

After countless attempts, the reboot was finally successful. I found myself standing in a hospital corridor. To my left was a gray-haired man in a lab coat. A stethoscope hung from his neck. To my right was a sweet looking woman.

"We're done here, Scott," the doctor said. "Your mom can take you home now."

No Mistakes

Two points of confusion immediately registered in my mind. First, I'd never seen this woman before in my life. How could she possibly be my mom? Second, why was the doctor calling me Scott? If there was one thing I knew—perhaps the only thing I was sure of—it was that my name was Kyle.

I took a good look at the woman, sizing her up from head to toe. What struck me most was the adoration in her eyes.

"Oh, honey," she said warmly, opening her arms to me.

I considered telling her the truth—that I had no idea who she was. Yet I feared doing this might have dire consequences. What would happen to me if I didn't embrace her as my mom? What would happen if I didn't go home with her? Did I have any other real options? She seemed so warm and loving. Maybe she really *was* my mom. Maybe something was wrong with me and that's why I was in the hospital.

The moment I stepped forward into her embrace, my whole body relaxed and my eyes filled with tears of joy. At the same time anxiety stirred in my belly. I felt as if I had just signed a contract binding me to be someone else for the rest of my life.

What would it take to be this Scott person? What if I slipped up at some point and Mom discovered the truth?

I'd have to become a diligent detective. I'd have to learn everything I could about Scottness so that I could properly fill his shoes. This work would require absolute vigilance, and the mere thought of beginning it was exhausting.

In the following days, weeks, and months I looked to everyone around me for clues to who I was. Sometimes I learned about Scottness through the confused look on a friend's face that suggested, *that doesn't seem like you*. Other times it was the wide eyes and enthusiasm that said, *yes, that's more like you!* Out of every expectation, every judgment, every story told about my past, I pieced together an identity based entirely on other people's perceptions of me. It was an exhausting process, and I often cried myself to sleep in the immense loneliness that my Kyle self felt deep down inside.

After months of living a lie, a tremendous tension had built up inside of me. I realized I didn't even like this Scott person, and living up to everyone's expectations of who I supposedly was was becoming increasingly onerous. More-over, I had begun to realize that most of the people around me had signed the very same contract I had: they too looked to everyone around them to define who they were. Almost everyone seemed to be just as lonely as I was.

My Scottness contract was breached one day during a baseball game. A guy on the other team threw me an off-handed insult. It didn't affect me much, but my buddies jumped into action. They positioned themselves between the heckler and myself. They put their hands up to block me.

"Let it go," one of them said. "He's just being an idiot."

"Don't do it, man!" another commanded. "You'll get thrown out of the game."

As I watched the situation unfold, I realized that I was supposed to break through the barrier they had formed to give the heckler a piece of my mind. I was supposed to do this with my fists. That's who I used to be.

For the first time since my new life had begun, I refused to be the Scott that everyone expected of me. I turned and walked away.

My friends now became the hecklers, calling me a wimp and suggesting that my gonads must have dropped off. A slow, cold shiver traveled down my spine as I realized that their statements were true, but not for the reasons they suggested. I had been a wimp since the moment I'd signed the imaginary contract inside myself and pretended to be someone I was not. Right there on the baseball diamond, I shredded the old contract and signed a new one. From that day forward I would remember my life from the inside out rather than the outside in. I would bring Kyle back to life.

|||||||

This incredible experience taught me that we are much greater than the stories our names, friends, and family members can tell of us. We are complex people. We are blooms fulfilling the seeds of consciousness that code us.

To fulfill the potential of our unique coding is a calling we cannot afford to ignore. And yet all the while we are pressured to act more like those around us, to be people we are not. It's a big task, and it isn't easy. We are often tempted to skirt the responsibility, opting instead to overwork, overeat, or become inebriated to avoid facing the task of discovering who we really are. But ultimately we all yearn to fulfill ourselves. That impulse never dies.

As an amnesiac, I was gifted with the conscious awareness of this strange struggle and the primal drive to overcome it. Decades later I found myself co-creating schools and writing books to help others engage with their true nature. One of my public schools was named Charter School of the Year in California. Why? Because children thrive when they are allowed to be true to themselves. When the curriculum centers around a student's unique interests and passions, learning unfolds as the great joy warranted to each of us by our human birthright.

Is it true that there are no accidents in life? Is it true that everything happens for a reason? I believe these statements *become* true when we make the conscious decision to use each experience in our lives—positive or negative—as an opportunity to learn and grow.

Here's to the spirit inside that drives us toward authentic fulfillment despite the forces that press against us. I now see a deeper meaning in that strange question that began my journey . . . *What time is it?*

It's time to wake up.

Winds of Love and Joy

ANNE M. DEATLY

Let all that you do be done in love.
—1 Corinthians 16:14

When the wind changes direction, new opportunities blow in.

For the past twenty-one years, I had worked at the same pharmaceutical company. And for twenty-one years the potential of looming mergers was constant. I survived several big mergers, but I was always wondering, *What would I do if I got laid off? Would I work at another pharmaceutical company doing similar research? Or would I teach and develop a research program at a university or medical school?* For years, I considered only these two options. The more specialized I became, the fewer opportunities I had to share my skills and knowledge.

Two years after the last merger, the whole environment at my company changed. Most people were laid off within the first year, and there was a constant cloud over the site. *Who would go next?* Some of my colleagues were showing signs of emotional unraveling. Professionalism waned. People got physically sick. Within a year, six people were diagnosed with cancer. The environment had become toxic emotionally and physically, but the stress just kept on building. More, more, more! We were supposed to feel lucky to still have jobs.

Some opportunities for career growth were eliminated during the consolidation phase, including my track in viral vaccine research, and like a sailboat stalled until the next gust of wind, I felt adrift. I was just waiting for the next executive decision to come down and determine my fate. It seemed pointless to set my own compass. I felt disempowered and windless.

As a PhD research scientist, I'd always loved discovering new things. Doing experiments and analyzing data brought me real joy, and I loved the challenge of organizing data and interpreting it to reveal meaning. But the stress of my job made me feel detached from my project and from the company's big picture, and I finally longed to do something completely different. I started to think of alternate career options.

Another experience weighed heavily on my mind during this time, propelling me along the path to change. I had lost my significant other to colon cancer a few years earlier, and I was smacked in the face with the reality of the limitations of Western medicine. Chemotherapy is only successful until your body develops a resistance to it. I began studying energy medicine in Donna Eden's certification program right around the time that big merger changed everything at work. Like positive charges flowing to me along a meridian pathway, I learned new skills and valuable, impactful techniques and exercises that revitalized my life. This gust of inspiration lifted me up, eventually guiding me to a new life and health paradigm.

I would come home from my research job and immerse myself in energy work. I became grounded, balanced, and energized. My new vibrancy and stamina affected not only how I lived my life, it also affected my beliefs. Suddenly the stress at work didn't seem to be worth it anymore. I saw how adversely it was affecting my coworkers and me, and despite liking the work I just couldn't justify staying any longer. A new life's purpose became very clear, and I realized that having the opportunity to be fully engaged and inspired was worth taking a chance on. With this new realization, I overcame my fears and made the decision to quit my job.

Once I was uplifted by this life change, I realized I could help lift up others with my new skills and knowledge. I started assessing the energies of family and friends, and correcting their energetic imbalances. I witnessed physical and emotional changes in people. They came to me stressed and fatigued and left vibrant, energetic, and ready to conquer the world! I was creating health and well-being!

My heart was fully engaged, and I radiated love and joy. With this sustained energy and stamina I understood at last what it meant to be optimally healthy.

Of course I don't regret my twenty-one years spent as a lab researcher. That part of my journey was invaluable in terms of bringing me to where I am today. Everything we do makes up an important part of who we are and who we will become. But I finally learned not to settle. I was separate from my true magnificence for a long time, but through following my energies and inspiration I rediscovered my passion. What resonates with your heart energy is your passion. Commit to this and there will be no mistakes.

When we are energetically balanced, we live our lives in perfect harmony. The winds of the world guide us to create heaven wherever we are—we just have to be in harmonic resonance. We have to set our sails and be prepared to move when the call beckons. We have to trust in the mystery of life and our intuitive passions. Through movement and trust, we can become the best version of ourselves.

Looking back, leaving my career as a PhD research scientist was actually much easier than I thought it would be. Remember, when it comes time to make radical changes in your life, there are no mistakes. You may not understand why you feel compelled to do what you do, but your heart will not lead you astray. When you send love to everything, love is what you receive in return.

Healing your life occurs at a different level of consciousness. My wish for you is that you will embrace your power and create the life of your dreams. You really can do anything you decide to do. As you sail through life, embrace the winds of growth and change. Fill your sails with a gust of fresh air and go for it! The world needs more people living their passions and connecting to their heart and soul. Step boldly into your new power of living and being, and commit to being your best. Open to joy, and radiate love out into the world. Vibrating at the frequencies of love and joy is what you need and what the world needs!

The Perfect Storm

ANN WHITE

We've all heard the expression "Be careful what you wish for," and I know this to be true firsthand. My wishes were truly answered, but not in a way I would have ever dreamed. The path took me through a life-altering medical and emotional journey, like falling through a dark tunnel and spiraling out of control until emerging into the light, safe and sound, exactly where I was meant to be.

Allow me to share my journey with you, from my prayers, through the abyss, and into the glorious life I now enjoy.

I've had some really high highs in my life, and some low lows, too. And for big portions of it I wasn't very happy. For fifteen years I was a divorce attorney, and I hated every day of it. How, you might ask, did I end up in a profession I hated from day one? Well, there was a series of events and

91

regrettable circumstances that led up to me deciding to get into divorce law. You could say it was a combination of two perfect storms happening ten years apart.

When I finished law school, I went into a profession that suited my soul as much as the air I breathe suited my body. I became an international management consultant. I traveled around the globe with a group of incredible colleagues solving corporate problems. Often our team would consist of an MBA, a PhD, and a JD (me). It was fun, heady, and I always loved the challenge and sense of accomplishment after finishing a project.

In 1980, one of my projects was to show that the Philippines was a safe destination for tourist travel. We flew to Manila for the job—I even met Philippine President Ferdinand Marcos and his wife, Imelda. I was very apprehensive about taking on this job, though, because the Philippines really was a tumultuous place at the time.

There was a terrorist bombing in Manila shortly after we arrived, and then some truly scary run-ins with the anti-Marcos militia. I had forewarning about there being a potential terrorist attack, and I had shared this information with my company, urging them to decline the project. But they insisted on moving forward, and I was sent into danger because, I suspect, they valued the high fee I was delivering more than my safety. The project failed, understandably, and this was the beginning of the first perfect storm in my life.

After the bombing, I was soured on my work and my company. Then I returned home to find my apartment had been burglarized of everything, even my pet cockatiel. I called the police, and when the cop came to take the report, he proceeded to back me into a corner and rape me. I was in shock. Whom do you call for help when something like this happens?

Afraid for my life and any repercussions of this incident, I quit my job and moved to the bucolic country in northwest Connecticut with a man I had been dating. We married a year later and had our son the following year. I enjoyed a thoroughly delightful life in this rural community doing some small grant projects and volunteering at the Legal Aid Society with domestic and sexual violence victims.

Then perfect storm number two happened: nearly ten years after storm one, my husband packed up a thirty-seven-foot motorhome and said, "I'm moving to Florida with or without you." That should have been my cue to stay in Connecticut, but I was thrown off by this flip announcement, and I immediately packed up my things, our son, and my dog and jumped into the motorhome and off we went.

In Florida I tried to find a job, any job that was not law. I'd taken the Florida bar just to have it as insurance, but it was clear that the adversarial nature of the practice of law was not conducive to my soul.

On my fortieth birthday, after less than a year in Florida, my husband made another announcement: "I have a girlfriend and I am moving out." And he did. There I was, barely forty, in a new state with no support system, a young son, and no job.

I cried for days. Then I went to several banks to see if I could get a job in their trust department since they hired attorneys. I was told by one, "Sorry, honey, but we do drug testing here." I guess I should have let my eyes recover from the tears before I went job hunting.

Finally, desperate, I heard there was a job opening at the Legal Aid office an hour from my home. Since I had volunteered at Legal Aid in Connecticut, I stormed the office saying that I was an attorney with Legal Aid experience and needed a job. I must have made some impression, because I started the next week.

And that's how I got into the practice of law. I left Legal Aid after five years and started my own practice and even became board-certified because I believe that whatever we do, we should do it to the best of our ability. But every day without exception, I prayed to God: "Get me out of here!"

I always thought there would be the perfect employment ad, or a call from someone asking me to take the perfect job. But that's not how it happened. Things had to get worse before they would get better.

In 2002, I needed to have a simple surgical procedure done, a bladder suspension with only a 1 percent chance of failure. Not bad odds, unless you are the 1 percent. Unfortunately for me, I was. Some nerves were damaged during the surgery, and I had to use a catheter for a year in order to urinate. After a year, I no longer needed the catheter, but I was incontinent; I had very little control over my bladder or my bowels.

I remember the first time I peed in court. I jumped up

from my chair during a trial and yelled, "Objection!" As pee ran down my legs into my shoes, I literally forgot what I was objecting to. No way could I stay in the practice of trial law when I kept leaking during a trial or even during a mediation.

During the last years of my practice I began studying Judaism, partly out of genuine interest, partly out of a desire to switch professions as my incontinence became a problem. When I finally could not practice law any longer, I got ordained as a rabbi and another door opened: I got a congregation in the same town where I practiced law. This worked well. During the service, I knew the parts where the cantor had a longer song and I could dart off the *bimah* (altar) and go to the bathroom. But my incontinence got worse, and I knew my time as a rabbi was coming to an end.

Then, with the synchronicities of a perfect storm in reverse, I got a job as a trauma/hospital chaplain. The perfect job. Do you know how many bathrooms there are in a hospital?

As a trauma/hospital chaplain, I am able to meet and impact so many wonderful people. I am with them at their lowest times, when life has dealt them a severe and devastating blow, and I am able to help them catch their breath and their balance as they find their center in the midst of their own storm. I love my job, and I've no doubt prepared for it well.

Never, ever would I have prayed for this journey as a way to leave the practice of law. "O God, please make me incontinent and thoroughly embarrassed so I can find a suitable job in a vastly different profession." In fact, when I first became incontinent, I thought I could not go on. I considered ending my life, but I still had my son, and shortly I adjusted and realized that I was OK and that this journey would be a wild ride but a worthwhile one. It is amazing what we can adjust to and turn to our advantage.

Life unfolds in its own way and in its own time, and though I had to make it through some rough, rough waters to get where I am today, I still trust that all is as it should be. Now, when I face uncertainty, I face it with curiosity rather than fear. For it is by looking for the growth or opportunity in each lesson that we begin to create the life we want to live. Be adaptable and listen to what you need, and the universe will provide.

Healing the Ghosts of the Past

LINDA WHEELER WILLIAMS

By the age of twenty-five, it was clear that my life had not
turned out as I had hoped. With my marriage ending, I had
to pick up the slack and get myself a job to support my two
children. I felt like I was thrown to the wolves with no experience in the world. I tried to provide a good life for my
family, but when I wasn't successful I became depressed, and
I even considered taking my own life. I couldn't understand
why things had turned out for me as they did, or why I felt
so miserable and lost.

I now realize that I was haunted by ghosts of my past.
And it was only through coming to terms with the demons
of my childhood that I was able to recover and move on with
my life. You see, my childhood was defined by two things: an
overcrowded house and a mother who didn't love me. The

summer of my sixth birthday we had about a dozen kids at our house every day. My mother had signed my father and herself up to be foster parents, and she also babysat during the day. During that time the Department of Children and Family Services did not have the policies it does now, and since responsible foster parents were hard to come by, my mother and father were eagerly accepted for what they did best—take care of other people.

Everyone in the neighborhood came to my mother for advice, support, loans, food, a place to stay, even a place to die. She and my father would take in family members and neighbors who were sick, had little money, and no one to care for them, and they had on occasion provided a burial for someone who couldn't afford one. We were always struggling financially, and I viewed these additional people at our house as the cause of it.

I used to watch my mother give so much comfort to these strangers, and I would think, "Why does she hate me so much?" I would look at pictures of my mother kissing and hugging me when I was a toddler and wonder what had happened.

Then, in second grade, I received a revelation that explained why I felt like an outcast. I was washing my hands in the girl's restroom when several of my classmates crowded around me and asked, "Did you know you were adopted?"

I remember scrubbing the soapy foam between my hands a little longer than I needed to, and then without looking up I answered, "Of course I knew that." And that was how I found out what it meant to be adopted. But I think inside I had already known.

As I grew older my mother would bully me and make me cry. She would tell me things like, "You are too weak," and "You wear your heart on your sleeve." This type of treatment went on for years, and I became more of a recluse. I found no joy in being around my family. Escaping into my room and into my fantasy world, traveling the world with the characters in my books, was my only respite.

Around age twelve I asked my mother why she had adopted me. She said, "I needed help around the house," and continued, "I don't even like kids!" I was crushed. She had just confirmed what I had feared all along: she really didn't love me.

When my mother passed years later, I was relieved. After all those miserable, torturous years that I'd wished she was dead, the day had finally come. I was really sad too, though, and I felt guilty. I cried alone in my bedroom, burying my face in my pillow, not wanting to upset my father or my kids. I had to be the strong one now. Fortunately, in the years preceding her death our relationship had improved. After I got married and had children of my own, my mother was more responsive. She adored her grandchildren, and they loved her too. It was a happy time for me; I felt that my mother finally accepted me.

But despite this improvement my past still haunted me, and my mother's passing, combined with my husband leaving me and the inevitable depression that followed that, showed me that these issues were not going away by themselves. I would have to take action to heal my past.

My first step was contacting Kentucky's adoption division, and I completed the paperwork to receive information on my biological mother. It took some time, but a year later I finally got the call that my biological mother wanted to see me. My heart jumped at the thought. For years, I had wished this fantasy birth mom would come and rescue me, and I would finally have someone who loved me. We spoke over the phone several times and finally met in person. I learned that she was from Scotland and was working in Chicago for a family on a work visa. She and my father had met in a restaurant where he worked. She was white and he was "colored," and in 1955 it was dangerous to have an interracial relationship, so they dated in secret. Then she got pregnant. The minister's wife of the church she attended noticed the pregnancy first, and after my mother confirmed the pregnancy she was taken to an unwed mothers home in Kentucky.

With her family in another country and out of reach, she had no visitors or packages. The other girls at the home taunted her. The only friend she had was the matron of the home. One evening, the matron told her not to worry, that her baby would have a nice home with a rich family in Kentucky. Knowing that she was pregnant by a colored man, she was afraid of what would happen once the baby was born. A few weeks before she was due, my mother finally told the matron.

As my biological mother suspected, this family was not interested in adopting a baby of color. But since they had already paid for the adoption and my mother's fare back to Scotland, they gave me to a couple that worked on their farm. And that was how I came to be with my adoptive mother. She took me when no one else would. My mother said that she served my adoptive mother and father lunch during an interview arranged by the adoption agency, and it gave her comfort to meet the couple who would be raising her child.

During our visits, I learned of a series of strange similarities between my biological mother and my adoptive mother: They shared the same name: Irene. They both had siblings named Margaret and James. Even more curious was the fact that my biological Aunt Margaret, who lives in Scotland, named her home Chevonna (they do that there, name their homes) and I had a baby girl named Shevonna. Both are pronounced the same way. These discoveries opened my eyes that maybe there was someone or something orchestrating my life.

I eventually met my biological sisters, and they had had an upbringing almost exactly the opposite of mine: they were affluent. They had the finest of everything growing up, and they traveled to different continents. Yet strangely, after hearing my sisters' stories about how they grew up, I somehow knew deep down inside that my adoptive family had been the best place for me.

Meeting my birth mother and half-sisters gave me a sense of closure, and I started working on my healing process to be free and at peace with my childhood. I forgave my adoptive mother whom I had hated for so long, and I forgave myself for those horrible feelings. I started remembering better times, like the beautiful lingerie she always wore, the calming smell of Noxzema, the delicious food she prepared, and how she always cheered for her favorite characters in movies or on television. These memories are what I dwell on now, and when the not-so-nice memories pop up, they don't smart as much anymore.

After seeking peace within, I realize that my adoptive mother actually loved me very much. I had compassion for her situation. She was raising a lot of kids all the time, and she loved me the best she was able to. I see now that she was my greatest teacher, because she prepared me to survive in a world she thought would be hard and take advantage of my kindness and soft heart.

After I arrived at this place of peace with my adoptive mother, I was able to see and understand things from her perspective. When I was young I would often watch her sleep, and sometimes she would cry and appear to be fighting. I wondered what she was dreaming about. I later learned that she had been raped when she was younger. Was that why she wouldn't allow me to go anywhere or stay out all night with other people when I was growing up? She wasn't just being strict; she was protecting me from threats I didn't know about yet, ones that she had experienced.

The more I looked, the more evident it became that my adoptive mother had loved me very much. By finally facing the memories of my past, my depression and self-loathing were lifted. I no longer am depressed or have thoughts of suicide.

Today I honor both of my mothers and the sacrifices they made. Through them, I have learned the gifts of compassion, love, and acceptance, and I am blessed to be able to share those gifts with my children each day as their mother.

Looking over my life, I have learned there are lessons we all have to experience that can be difficult even when you understand how the universe works. No matter what has happened in the past, no matter what you are going through right now, remember that you can overcome it. It's all about having the courage to trust yourself, trust your life process, and believe that there is a greater plan in the works to benefit you and your highest good.

The Art of Taking the High Road

CLIFF THOMAS

The day that my now ex-wife and I told our kids that we were getting divorced will forever be etched in my brain. I saw those angelic, innocent faces distorted and sobbing as they faced something way too harsh for their beautiful minds to process. I made a vow that I would do anything and everything in my power to be the best father I could be for them. As a result, that day I decided I would always take the high road. While I have faltered at times, that mind-set is the lighthouse that keeps my ship headed in the right direction.

My ex and I had a collaborative divorce, and as part of the process the court ordered us to participate in a group counseling session. We went together and sat together. We listened intently as the counselor spoke about how most children who come from divorced families are damaged, and only 10 percent grow stronger from the experience. I knew that our children were passengers on this divorce journey and that my ex-wife and I were in the driver's seat. Our actions and behaviors would influence whether they would be in the 90 percent that were damaged or the 10 percent that grew stronger. When my children were sobbing I knew emotionally why I would always take the high road; now I knew the practical reason.

Then I asked the counselor, "What do children need to grow strong as their parents are going through a divorce?" From the counselor's response four points stuck with me as being the most important. He said children need: a low-tension environment, reassurance that they are safe and secure, love, and the opportunity to experience childhood adventures.

Providing a safe and secure environment was easy for me. There was no abuse, and my income was enough to easily provide a secure home and neighborhood. Frankly, love was easier after my divorce, because when my children were with me, it was all me. In the beginning, I think they could have asked for any gift and I would have run out to buy it for them. But I quickly realized that was not the kind of love I wished to share. I wanted to share my heartfelt love, not the love of a Disneyland dad. So I planned adventures for us. We would do things like camp and go on hikes and talk.

About one year after the divorce I took my children to Canada. The plan was to fly into Vancouver and then take a float plane to a secluded lake a couple hours north of Whistler and camp, explore, canoe, hike, and fish. We landed in Vancouver late at night and went to bed. We had the next day to explore the city before leaving for Whistler, and we needed to get up and get moving.

As I was trying to get the kids up and packed, my daughter was lying on the bed, awake but groggy, and I tossed a computer toward her to pack. It hit the bed, slid, and hit her. Oh my gosh, you would have thought that I had beat her severely. She began crying and ran off to the bathroom to call her mother. The conversation was easy to hear through the bathroom door, and what I heard made me mad. On principle, I knew that I could not control the behavior of my ex, and I knew she meant well. But emotionally, I wanted to prove that what I did was OK and the conversation my ex was having was not OK. I knew that any intervention in the conversation would have produced tension, though, so I took a deep breath and then let it go. It was times like this that I found creating a low-tension environment challenging.

But all's well that ends well. My kids have great memories of that day spent carelessly exploring Vancouver, and the camping was off-the-charts fun and created stories that had nothing to do with divorce.

|||||||

I loved my ex-wife, not as a husband would, but as a person who knew how beautiful her soul was and how difficult a time this was for her. I understood that I could not control her actions and should avoid any attempts to do so. So instead of allowing myself to fight over an unimportant issue, I forced myself to step back and ask myself, "What are my principles?"

As a man, my first response was to approach divorce as a war with my ex, a battle between the masculine and the feminine. Under the extreme stress of the emotional storm of divorce, I wanted to make it all logical, which contrasted greatly with her feminine desire to express things in emotional terms. Keeping this in mind, I knew I needed to take a moment and step away from a situation any time I felt like a fight was brewing. Allowing myself a few moments of peace allowed me to better keep my resolution to always take the high road.

In the early days of divorce, I experienced lots of changes, and even the simple ones hurt intensely. I missed the simple things, like my chair in the living room or at the dinner table, my yard, my kitchen, and the changed relationships with friends that resulted from our separation. I missed the everyday routines with my ex and my kids. Now there were new living arrangements, new bills, and new challenges.

I learned to embrace these emotions and then act on my principles of integrity. I learned what my principles were by stepping back and asking myself, "Am I physically, financially, and emotionally capable of doing this, and will it benefit my children?" Interestingly, this shifted the battle away from my ex and her behavior to my own behavior. When I was successful, I felt proud of my behavior. When I faltered, as I have many times, I came back to the mind-set *always take the high road.*

Along with these changes and challenges, divorce also opened up the opportunity for me to learn more about myself. I learned more about my limiting beliefs, my fears, my concerns, strengths and weaknesses, and it gave me time to find out what I loved and rediscover my passion and purpose in life.

I am happy to report that this strategy helped me turn one of the most painful experiences of my life, a divorce, into a positive way of living that has impacted every relationship I have. My job is to always take the high road.

From the Dark Night of the Soul to the Dawn of Spiritual Breakthrough

KAREN HASSELO

I sat alone on the hardwood floor in my kitchen in total darkness, replaying the pronouncement earlier in the day: my only child, whom we had longed for, had autism. What factors had conspired to kidnap my charming, beautiful, blue-eyed, towheaded toddler, leaving behind this mute, eyes-glazed-over imposter? I not only lost the child I had hoped for, but many of my long-term friends grew distant and eventually disappeared shortly after my son's diagnosis.

Four years later, my twenty-year marriage disintegrated. All my hopes and carefully crafted plans invested in this relationship became defunct, and I was forced to leave the dream home we inhabited. Within months my former husband married a much younger woman. During a quiet moment, I asked myself, "Has my life truly become a cliché?"

Not long after my separation, I left my job of sixteen years in order to be a stay-at-home therapist for my son and full-time trainer and supervisor of other home therapists. It was during this time that I developed an incapacitating chronic illness, and my son was diagnosed with childhood bipolar disorder in addition to autism.

All these experiences were thrown together in such a brief window of time that I was thrust into the dark night of the soul. I became conditioned to my aloneness, my separation from my God-Source, and entrenched in blaming others or myself. I slowly nursed my internal story of devastation, bitterness, and despair.

Up until this point in my life, I had masked my fear by being a perfectionist, an overachiever, and a workaholic. I was ultra-controlling and detail-oriented—someone who always tried to "steer the river." I was attached to preconceived outcomes, and my trust in the Divine was dependent upon me getting what I demanded. My body had become a physical manifestation of my empty spiritual and emotional landscape.

It felt as though I would never escape what the universe had done to me, until one night when I heard guidance whispering from somewhere deep inside of me, barely audible against the backdrop of doubts, fears, and victim stories that

I continuously told myself. The guidance said to me, "All of your attempts to control the people and circumstances of your life are futile. They represent resistance, a 'no' to life." Though I'll never know how I found the courage, at that moment I made a decision to say yes to life.

After that initial *yes* that night, I found my spirit was somehow lifted, and it became easier to go on. I embraced the empowerment inherent in the word *yes*. I said yes to each and every opportunity that presented itself. One night, in a dream my guides told me that healers from the other side were working for my highest good, but it would be up to me to take full responsibility for my own healing. I said yes, and within a few short months I unexpectedly crossed paths with a perfect stranger who referred me to my first holistic practitioner. This chiropractor worked tirelessly to treat me over the next ten years.

Although I was still homebound due to my chronic illness, I said yes to a Reiki master who was willing to make a home visit. During my session, while my eyes were closed, my guides presented a massive phoenix flying out of a valley and circling below the cloud break. I interpreted this vision as a gift of hope and sustenance. While I only saw this healer three times, he became the conduit for putting me in the hands of a most skilled medical intuitive who has played a very significant role in bringing me even further into the light.

Through my own concerted efforts in partnership with all my healers, one year ago I was given back the life-force energy to say yes to training to become a spiritual life coach. This gift in and of itself is a miracle for a woman who has spent much of the last thirteen years bedridden. I am in transition, learning to focus less on my fear-based thoughts, my old defense mechanisms, and the personas I act out, and more on connecting with who I truly am—a divine being who has incarnated to have a most human experience. I am learning to release the core negative beliefs and the emotional anchors that have kept me from realizing my divine potential.

I am learning to surrender to any circumstance, knowing that all has been perfectly designed. When I embrace *yes* while listening to my intuitive self, I move into alignment with the flow of my life. Every experience gives me a new opportunity to demonstrate the emotional courage to own my personal truths, even when I am in resistance. When I am in resistance, I am creating more of what I have already experienced. I can now see that I created past experiences with my resistance to certain situations; and I remind myself that surrender, saying yes, is what brought me out of that dark night of the soul.

The antidote to resistance is surrender, and when I turn my circumstances over to Universal Love, I know that I can trust that all my experiences are designed to help me build my spiritual muscles for the purpose of spiritual growth.

At the beginning of this journey, I believed that my life's work was to "rescue my son" from autism. Little did I realize that my son would become my catalyst and master teacher, placed here to deliver me from the negativity that I had created and surrounded myself with. Through allowing myself to open to a higher level of consciousness, to surrendering and simply saying yes to whatever situation might arise, I grew to accept that if I chose my own reality, I was a potential visionary; not a victim. None of this would have been possible if it weren't for my dark night of the soul, which ultimately led to my spiritual breakthrough.

A Lesson from an Angel

MANDY BERLIN

It was Christmas Eve, and my friend Nancy and I had just taken my mom to the mall to have her hair done before we all went out to dinner.

Suddenly my mother collapsed and screamed out in pain, "My back!"

As she lay on the cold concrete floor, I cried and stroked her cheek as we waited for the medical personnel to arrive from the hospital across the street. Now instead of going home with us to celebrate Christmas, my beautiful mother was being taken to the hospital.

Soon old thoughts pulsed in my brain, thoughts of my beloved husband Max dying of cancer only three hours before Christmas Eve several years prior. How could I possibly grasp this terrible coincidence?

All I wanted to do in that moment was help my poor mother. But how could I help her? I did not know. Then I heard a deep, reassuring voice from within my soul say, "The hows are the domain of the universe!"

Right after I heard that awe-inspiring voice, my mind went to one of the fundamental laws of the universe, the Law of Attraction, which, stated simply, is that like attracts like.

According to the Law of Attraction, everything in the universe has a vibrational frequency. Your vibrational frequency is created by your brain through your thoughts and associated feelings, like joy, sorrow, fear, gratitude, anger, and the highest frequency of all, love.

The Law of Attraction states that the vibration you transmit is the vibration you will, in due course, receive (like a boomerang effect!). You create your world consciously when you articulate your desires—through your dominant thoughts, feelings, and beliefs—and allow them to come to fruition. And belief is imperative. If you doubt that you will receive something, you never will until you change your vibration to belief.

I had been practicing and teaching the Law of Attraction to friends and loved ones for several years at that point, and I knew from experience that whenever I employed attraction with intent and belief, amazing things had happened. So the night my mother fell, I made a crucial decision: I was going to use the Law of Attraction to help her. I had to believe that she was going to be well.

As my mother slept in a hospital bed, her doctor said,

"We cannot replace your mother's pelvic bone because she is elderly. No surgery is possible. I'm sorry, Mandy, but it does not look good." I shook my head soberly, but in my mind I promptly dismissed this medical fact. "I must stand in faith," I thought. "Stay focused on the good."

That night Nancy and I returned to my home, and I sat up in bed and remembered an enlightening book I'd read by Sunny Dawn Johnston: *Invoking the Archangels: A Nine-Step Process to Heal Your Body, Mind, and Soul*. During the month of Thanksgiving, I had reread and studied the invocations, especially the prayer to the awesome healer Archangel Raphael. I decided to use that prayer now to bring healing and peace to my mother.

Before dawn the next morning, I prayed to Raphael for my mom to be healed in body, mind, and soul. Then I wiped my eyes and said, "Dear Raphael, if you can hear my prayer, would you please give me a sign?" A moment later, the fire alarm beeped—five short bursts. It was loud and powerful enough to even wake Nancy in the next room. But there was no fire, and no apparent explanation for why the fire alarm had beeped. I knew it was Archangel Raphael letting me know he had heard my prayer! And on that lovely Christmas morning, I got up and traced the flakes of frost on the window, all the while knowing my mother would live.

Still, the path would not be easy. Over many weeks, I saw my dear mother fight through terrible pelvic pain and complications. She suffered two bouts of the highly contagious and dangerous virus MRSA and had to be moved to the isolation ward. But I kept my mind centered on healing, and I prayed for her, as did our friends. When I had to leave the hospital, I would "visit" Mom by phone and teach her the healing techniques of attraction. And before she went to sleep at night, we would recite Sunny's invocation to Archangel Raphael. I felt my body being lifted, hovering with Raphael above my mother's bed. And with his kind, loving guidance, I taught my mom how to heal herself.

The second time I visited my mother, the doctors said that if she pulled through it would take twelve to fourteen weeks for her pelvic bone to heal. Mom's pelvic bone healed in only ten weeks, and even the MRSA virus she had contracted miraculously cleared up the day before we had planned to take her home to live in Arizona.

Now, my mom is walking every day, with a cane and a smile. We live our lives in abundance, going out to parks, gatherings, and dinner every week. Since 2006, when I seriously began to apply the Law of Attraction, I have considered it to be a vital part of my life, and I have dedicated many hours to studying and teaching people how to apply the law to their lives to create healing, harmony, and tranquility. But I never imagined that it would so greatly impact my life. My mother's accelerated recovery could only have come about by focusing our thoughts and prayers on the positives that surrounded us and by adhering to the beautiful certainty within. By using the Law of Attraction and invoking the Archangel Raphael to help my mother to heal herself, I have truly experienced the power of this law and the infinite potential of the spirit. I am still in awe of the boundless capacity we possess to change our lives, in body and in spirit, with just a simple redirection of the mind.

Trauma and New Beginnings

SARA JANE

At thirty-eight, I had a wisdom tooth extracted and my jaw was broken in the process. It took a two-hour operation to push the jaw bone back into place and attach a plate to hold the bones together. In that same year my second marriage ended, and a corporate merger at work threatened the security of my job.

Somehow I found an inner strength and determination to face these challenges. After all, I had spent most of my life depending on no one but myself following an earlier stay in the hospital. At only one year old, an accident involving scalding hot milk left me with burns on my face and throat, plus the jumper I had been wearing had stuck to the skin of my lower neck. I was admitted to the hospital right away.

Unfortunately, at the time, parents were not allowed to

stay with their children in the hospital, and even visiting hours were very limited. The result was that for the three months I was in the hospital, at a time when I was in pain and desperately needed the comfort of cuddles and the soft, loving tones of Mummy's voice, there was nothing.

Because of this, I grew up feeling very insecure and unloved. I felt I wasn't good enough at people-pleasing behavior, and my attempts to make myself into someone people could love would fail. For the next thirty-seven years, my motto became, "If you don't love, you can't get hurt."

Perhaps this helps to explain why the hardest part of my broken jaw and oral surgeries ordeal wasn't the surgeries themselves, or even the painful week without a diagnosis that preceded it. The hardest part was the six months of pain and sleepless nights that followed; sleepless nights that, ironically enough, would be my wake-up call.

Painkillers and sleeping pills did not provide any relief, and exhaustion set in. I was so tired that I didn't have the energy to pretend anymore; my concentration on what others may be thinking, what they might want, took too much effort. And for the first time since I was a toddler, all my energy went to just being myself—it was all I could manage. And whether people liked that person or not was of no concern to me.

Strangely enough, once I gave myself permission to look for answers about why I had shut myself down to feeling love, three things occurred to me:

1. I had no idea what others were really thinking or feeling. How could I make myself responsible for fulfilling all their hopes and dreams when I had no way of knowing what they were? Yes, I could guess, but I was trying to do the impossible.

2. In the majority of cases, most people weren't even thinking about me simply because there was bound to be something more important happening in their lives.

3. If someone didn't like something I said, it was most likely due to something that was going on in their own life, and the interpretation they put on what I said. I never intend to mean any offense; and I have no control over what people hear—I only have control over what I say.

What a relief! With these realizations, I was suddenly free to make my own choices about my life. And with my marriage ending and my job being cut, there was nothing to keep me in the town where I lived. So, when opportunities arose, I simply started to say yes.

Now I feel like I fully participate in my life, which has changed beyond all recognition. I even signed up for an expedition to Romania with the Scientific Exploration Society (SES) in conjunction with the Carpathian Large Carnivore Project (CLCP) to track (not kill) wolves and lynx in the Carpathian Mountains! From there, I became a trainee handler of the wolves at the UK Wolf Conservation Trust.

I wanted to give back to my community, to share my blessings with others, and that came in the form of working with and befriending adults with learning difficulties. For the first time, I genuinely felt I was making a difference.

I actually feel blessed that my jaw was broken during a routine oral surgery. Otherwise, I wouldn't have been able to take back control of my life. I have since moved to a different town, met a wonderful group of friends, and found Reiki and other healing modalities. I have even set up my own practice, and I am now an international speaker on the healing and empowering energy of sound and the use of toning with the voice.

Every challenge is a gift that you can share with others. Open yourself to the challenges and experiences life has to offer, and you will allow yourself to learn and grow. There is no such thing as a wasted experience—or a mistake. The universe knows what it is helping you to achieve, even if you don't like how it is doing it. Believe me, you may not like how the universe is guiding you, it may even be painful—but even broken jaws can serve a good and higher purpose.

I spent thirty-seven years being afraid of my own shadow. Before, I would never have contradicted anyone, and certainly not done anything so different from the norm. But now I live my life in abundance, and my success is more profound than financial rewards. I am able to participate in my own life, accept the opportunities (and challenges) that come, and make them work for me. And most importantly, I am able to show others how to be true to themselves by example.

The Gift of Perspective
Propel Your Way to No Regrets

JANET ROZZI

If you were to tell my twenty-year-old self that standing outside in twenty-degree weather holding a coffee can to collect donations for families battling childhood cancer would someday directly benefit my family, I'd have said that was impossible. Things like cancer happened to other families, not mine. Years later, my sister would become a pediatric oncology nurse at the children's hospital where these brave young hearts receive treatment; surely she would know how to escape the same fate. As if knowing about cancer can prevent it.

My nephew, Andrew, was just three years old when my sister prayed that she was being an overreactive mother. But the spots on his joints would be a confirmed symptom of leukemia. Things had looked promising a year and a half after his first round of chemotherapy, and Andrew fought hard, but eventually the cancer started to cause his organs to deteriorate. He relapsed one night before Easter and was gone before Mother's Day.

I remember his last day with us vividly: harsh fluorescent lighting, the Andrea Bocelli CD (one of his favorites) playing in his hospital room, the lost look in my sister's eyes when she and her husband decided it was finally time to unplug the oxygen machine and allow him to drift into the peaceful beyond. It was a snapshot in time that would change me forever.

I couldn't grasp how my sister had the strength to go back to work on the same children's hospital floor and face the room that Andrew had called home for so long. However, she could now offer not just sympathy but true empathy to the families who were struggling to find their way through their new version of normal. My sister's resolve astounded me, and I longed to find the meaning in how something so devastating could happen to a family as wonderful as hers.

Andrew passed just three months before he was to be the ring bearer at our wedding. Somehow, my sister and her husband championed us through our wedding preparations, helping us with invitations, decorations, favors, and countless other tasks. They were selfless cheerleaders with a faith that was unshakable.

Two more years would pass before I had the grace to learn what they already knew: that even in our darkest hour there is a gift and a blessing, although many times it is well-disguised. It would take the stage-four bladder cancer diagnosis of my father, coupled with a miscarriage three months into my pregnancy (after trying for more than two years to get pregnant), to plunge me into ink-like darkness, then thrust me back out again. In the moment that I defiantly told my father that he didn't get to write himself off and avoid chemotherapy so he could wait to die comfortably, that he would be leaving those who loved him, it finally hit me—it wasn't about the darkness, the sadness, the loss. It wasn't about dying. It was about *living.* The thought of waiting around to die made me mad. Why not make the most of every moment while we're still here? There is a beautiful lesson that one very special angel boy taught my family: your world can change in an instant, so truly appreciate and make the most of what you have today.

We've all heard this advice before—*carpe diem;* you only live once; never put off till tomorrow what you can do today. But there's something about a crisis that changes everything. Somewhere within the swirl of chaos is a pivotal moment that changes you forever. What was *your* moment? Most likely, it was the instant when you suddenly had a new perspective on everything, from where you work to the people you call friends.

The clarity you experience puts every facet into perspective. Time is finite. You have dreams, passions, goals. You have a redefined purpose. How you get there is of no consequence, but the decision to take the first step is critical. It's how you are able to propel your way to no regrets. When you realize that hardship can birth you into a new perspective where you are ready to make the change that will propel you forward on a new path, you can almost feel a divine hand pushing you forward in that moment of clarity.

The blessing I received from the culmination of suffering the loss of my nephew and my unborn child, plus my father's life-threatening illness, was the resolve to live with no regrets. No more coulda, woulda, shoulda. Instead, I say, "Why not?" I now try to live every day knowing that I might only have today; I savor every moment and choose to live a purpose-driven life.

Living with the end in mind gives you a unique perspective. What are *you* going to worry about when you are lying on your deathbed, reflecting on your life? Perhaps it will be more about what you *didn't* do than what you did do.

Perspective is a gift. You have the ability to make the decision to be happy or sad about your circumstances, and you will always be able to find someone who's a bit worse off than you. The beauty in every experience is that it has brought you to exactly where you are today; any one change, and you might become someone else entirely.

I was blessed to learn at the young age of thirty-one to look for the lesson in every experience. Each loss, disappointment, and new experience has taught me about who I am as a person, and thus who I want to become. It's how my job has become an *offering of service* to others, how my friends have become *trusted advisors,* and how my life has become my *adventure.* The trick is to pay attention and look for the gift and blessing in every situation.

I now pay attention. What is my lesson, and what does it mean to me? I set a goal to make a difference in the world, so I followed my passion to help animals and focused on the service aspect of my career. I make more time for my family. I'm thrilled to share that my father is now cancer-free; every moment spent with my family and friends has become more precious than ever, something I will never again take for granted.

It's easy to get stuck in the vortex of drama and stress. But by consciously deciding to step out of the chaos, you are able to view the complete picture and see the lesson an experience is trying to teach you. You gain valuable perspective, which helps you to choose differently next time, to set different goals or boundaries.

The gift is learning to not wait until you are lying on your deathbed to discover what you want for your life. The gift is yours. Now, what are you going to do with that information? Hopefully you'll share it with others and help propel them into a life without regrets!

From Depression and Despair to Divine Love and Acceptance

TENAYA ASAN

I sobbed every day for three weeks. I couldn't stop the flood of tears. I felt like I was in a deep well with no way out, and no help on the horizon. Nothing I did had any impact on the sadness, frustration, and anxiety. I didn't know why I felt so miserable; there was no real crisis I could point to except that I had tried for years to ease my pain and nothing was working. I was at the end of the line. Every day when I returned home from work I would sit down and the tears would flow. Once I started crying I couldn't stop, and at times it went on for hours. My sobs were soon joined by pleas for help. I wanted to be closer to God. I wanted to be peaceful. If only I could find someone to teach me how to be closer to God, perhaps I could find solace.

At twenty-six, I moved to California looking for relief. I hoped to explore New Age thinking and to be in a place where being a gay woman was not an oddity—or at least where I could find others who did not see it as a psychosis. I liked people, and being an outsider was difficult for me. I was wound up so tightly that a simple "No, I have other plans tonight and can't go to the movies with you," from a friend could trigger feelings of insecurity and rejection for days.

I didn't have problems finding friends or lovers. I just had problems keeping them. Truly, I didn't know that my emotional reactivity was a problem. I felt perfectly justified in feeling anger or rejection. In my eyes, it wasn't me who was a problem—it was always "them."

As it turns out, there is now a diagnosis for the extreme hypersensitivity and reactivity that I experienced. It has been discovered that children who grow up in traumatic emotional or physical conditions have similar symptoms, now termed complex post-traumatic stress disorder (or complex PTSD). I was abused as a child, and I grew up with a parent who drank regularly and often threatened suicide. After growing up in this environment, I had a classic case of complex PTSD.

Unfortunately, no one understood complex PTSD at the time, and all the therapy, meditation, new-thought religion, and self-help seminars did not make a dent in the emotional anxiety and torment I experienced.

Then one day I was talking to a friend at a church I attended, and he mentioned an enlightened woman whom he had just met in San Francisco. My eyes lit up and my heart almost leaped out of my chest. I had an immediate feeling that she was my teacher, and I hoped that it was so!

Two weeks later I met Mara, a woman in her late thirties with dark hair and brown eyes that gazed with love that penetrated to the deepest reaches of my soul. Just one evening with Mara convinced me that my search was over. My heart and soul felt they had come home. There was no doubt, she was an old soul with wisdom and love beyond anyone I had ever known or could have imagined.

I became her student and did everything I could to be near her. In her company I felt at ease and joyful, as if life were magical. I felt loved. "Yes, this is how life is supposed to be!" I thought. She talked about women's conditioning and how to break through it and stand free. She taught us meditation and our true nature as stillness. But mostly she taught by example, living as a free woman, loving and being in the world but not of it, able to discriminate the conditioning and lies that we live with humor, clarity, and forthrightness that often rendered me speechless. Outdoor adventures, hikes, caravan trips, creative projects, long talks, and living together in community all served as her theater for engaging her small band of students in a practice of heart-focused attention.

But much to my dismay, the pure joy and innocence of being with Mara did not last. We, her students, were so starved for real love and so convinced that love resided with Mara, and not in our own hearts, that we became competitors against one another, often trying to convince her that we deserved her attention over the others. Like children vying for the teacher's love and attention, all of our worst behaviors were exposed. Time would reveal that I, among all of the students, would display some of the most hurtful behavior. Despite my almost impossible kindness to the master, my underhanded manipulation to try to earn her approval and attention put me at odds with the other students (and Mara herself). And thus, I received lots of correction!

For me, correction was equivalent to rejection and meanness. It triggered self-righteousness, self-pity, and self-criticism. But as much as I tried to convince Mara of my innocence, it was in vain. And as much as I tried to convince myself of her rejection, I found it impossible to imagine her feeling anything other than love and acceptance for me—even when I screamed at the top of my lungs, "You're mean! Stop hurting me!"

The next six years of my life were an ordeal of facing anxiety, anger, competition, extreme defensiveness, manipulative behavior, sadness, fear, blame, and yes, overwhelming joy and love that kept me in the community in spite of having little idea why I was so often pinpointed as the problem. Mara used every tactic she could imagine to help me.

At times my harsh behavior toward other students led her to exclude me from gatherings or living in the community household for a period of time. And then, for whatever reason, there were long reprieves when I lived in harmony with the community and with myself.

I certainly was not the only person who struggled with

correction. At a gathering near the end of those six years, Mara asked each of her students whom they felt hurt by the most. They all pointed to me. But as I heard and took in their scornfulness, remarkably, for the first time in my life I did not recoil or snap back with self-righteous anger.

Just two days before, in a Christmas Eve meditation with Mara, I had let go and found peace. It was then that I realized it was in letting go and not trying to manipulate my environment and those around me that I would find the peace I yearned for. For the first time in my life, I consciously understood and knew how to let go of physical and emotional tension and contraction and to melt into the exquisite stillness that is always present.

When each student said that I was the one they felt most hurt by, I had no response except to let go and relax. There was no anxiety, no need to argue, or run, or try to change the truth of what they felt. My only experience was excitement and joy in understanding that peace was possible through letting go and forgiving myself and others. I looked forward to the journey.

I stayed with Mara for another twelve years, and I will always hold her deep in my heart.

I am close to sixty now, and I can say that I truly know peace. I have a loving relationship, and I treasure myself and my life. I know it was no accident that I suffered an emotional breakdown early in my life, and that my quest to end my suffering led me to Mara and her community. Despite the heartache and troubles I both suffered and caused, divine guidance brought me to the one person whose strength, love, and wisdom could hold me to her, until I could finally unwind the knots of pain around my heart and find my way toward true and lasting peace.

The Power of Surrender

Patricia Cohen

It was the middle of the night and I was violently retching and couldn't catch my breath. As I reached for the bathroom door I thought, *God, if you make me stop throwing up I promise to serve you forever.* Before my hand touched the door I stopped throwing up. I felt a sense of peace and calm in my core. *Guess now I have to serve God forever—I wonder what that means.* I was just five years old though, and I knew I had some time to figure it out.

The next year at school I decided I would become a nun. I went to Catholic school, and at the time becoming a nun seemed like the natural progression on the road to serving God. It was easy to imagine too because I adored my first grade teacher, Sister Edwardine. My desk was at the front of the class and she gave me atomic fireballs for answering questions correctly and being good in class. She had a stash of them in some mysterious pocket in her habit. My hand was always up first to answer questions, and Sister Edwardine kept up her end of the deal, keeping those fireballs coming.

I loved going to mass with my class, and on Sundays I got to hear Sister Edwardine and my cousin Robin sing in the choir. I could tell their voices from the others because they sang like angels, and I felt like I was in heaven whenever I heard them sing.

I had my First Communion in that church when I was seven, and, shortly after, Sister Edwardine was transferred to another parish. One Easter Sunday I went to mass with my aunt and her family in Los Angeles and I heard Sister Edwardine singing in the choir. After mass I looked around frantically, and finally I spotted her in a gaggle of nuns walking out of the church. I ran up to her like I was running into the arms of my guardian angel. I knew she loved me too; I could feel it. We were so happy to see each other, and I cried for joy.

When I was eleven I went to visit my girlfriend after school, as I often did. One evening it was time to go home for dinner and my friend's brother asked if I wanted a ride. He was popular, black-haired and brown-eyed, with a smile that curled up on one side. I thought it was strange he wanted to give me a ride home because it was only a couple blocks away and I could probably run home faster than he could drive, but I agreed anyway.

Once we were in the car he stopped halfway between his house and mine and molested me. I didn't know what was happening, and I was so petrified I couldn't move. My throat closed up. I couldn't talk.

No one had discussed anything like that with me before, and I was afraid that if I told one of my six brothers I would be beat up or punished in some way. My parents were divorced and way too preoccupied with their own drama to know what was happening to me, and his parents only spoke Spanish, so I couldn't tell them either.

How do you talk about something when the words you need to use are forbidden? Even more devastating was the thought that I could no longer hope to become a nun, so I didn't know how I could serve God. The whole plan I had for my life fell away like shards of a broken flute, and there was nothing I could do about it. It was done. I felt lost and empty, and I believed I had let God down pretty badly.

When my parents divorced my father moved away and my mother went to college full-time and worked as a waitress at night and on the weekends. The eldest child had to care for the younger ones as there were no parents in the home most of the time, which meant there were eight wild children running the neighborhood. When my four older brothers left home it was my turn to babysit. I had to walk straight home from school to make sure everybody else got home, did their chores, and didn't kill each other, and I had to have dinner on the table when our mother got home at five o'clock.

Even though I was the fastest sprinter on the track team, and one of the best hurdlers, I was cooking, cleaning, and caring for children, and I had no social life unless my friends came over to see me. One time one of the girls in the neighborhood brought over a boy who was on leave from the Air Force to meet me. He was only a little taller than I was and had almost white-blonde hair. He was tanned and muscular from his training as a paratrooper. I fell in love on sight.

When he returned to Fort Bragg he asked me to marry him. I told my mother I was getting married, and she just said, "Oh!" So I went from the Mojave Desert to Fort Bragg and became a mother, cooking, cleaning, and soon caring for my own child, just like that.

Then tragedy struck again. Shortly before my sixteenth birthday my seven-week-old son died during the night. I was devastated, and I was angry at God. "What were you thinking, giving me a child I didn't ask for and then taking him away again so soon?" I hated God, and my hate was consuming. I became an atheist and actually spent many years using or abusing alcohol and other substances as a result.

Then one day, while walking along the Sierra Highway in the Mojave Desert, it struck me that it wasn't possible to hate something that didn't exist. I realized that if I hated God that must mean that I also believed in God. It was at that moment that I surrendered.

"I have no idea what you are thinking," I said to God, "but you must know." I instantly felt that same peace and calm in my core I had felt when I talked to God when I was just five years old. All the hate melted away and transformed into a desire to have more children and build a successful life of my own.

I knew there had to be a better way to raise a family than what I had seen around me growing up. I began a life of exploration, education, and observation. There were some important classes along the way that brought the pieces of my life back together into a beautiful chalice, a holy grail. For example, I was greatly influenced by a class developed by the Search Institute on the forty developmental assets kids need to succeed. I found the lessons offered through this course life-changing.

Now, I am in a position to consider what happened to me that day when I was eleven years old. Who knows what abuses and infringements the young man who violated me had suffered. I now believe that abuse is preventable if the needs of individuals are met physically, emotionally, and spiritually, if children are educated in what is expected and what is unthinkable and are given the love and support critical to us all.

I realized that unbelievable acts that hurt others are completely preventable, and I began writing about it. I would go on to work in the juvenile system as a corrections officer, devoting myself to a career of helping children in need. During this time I noticed something important: none of the children there had experienced coming-of-age traditions or other rites of passage. Kids need these rites of passage for a healthy upbringing; they're crucial.

I noticed that rites of passage are progressive throughout life, are individually experienced, and have inherent value. There are currently only a few groups of people using rituals and ceremonies for rites of passage, but everyone who experiences them benefits. My current career involves working with families to develop rites of passage traditions for their children by building on something most of us celebrate already: birthdays! Each birthday is a ceremony, a time to honor each person individually. Each birthday is a rite of passage. Adding a simple layer to the ceremony, like adding a layer to the cake, is the ideal opportunity to honor that person in their passage through life, and it provides an opportunity to strengthen them, which strengthens the chain of humanity.

As I look back, I have come a long way from the little girl whose family life crumbled when her parents divorced and she felt she couldn't turn to anyone when a neighbor molested her and she suffered the loss of a newborn, all before the age of sixteen.

But it was these events, and my initial rebellion to them, that led to my spiritual realization in the California desert. Once I embraced the power of surrender, I was transformed. Free from the all-consuming hatred and blame for the tragedies in my past, I was able to educate myself and have a strong family of my own, and I have since devoted my life to the service of others.

And to think, my plan was to be a nun.

Are You Part of My Tribe?
The Intelligence of Pattern Recognition

KIMBERLY BURNHAM

What do science fiction writer Isaac Asimov, actress Geena Davis, three-year-old Emmelyn Roettger, and even the animated character Lisa Simpson have in common? Membership in Mensa, which "fosters human intelligence for the benefit of humanity." Many Mensa questions are based on pattern recognition and determining what does or doesn't fit. For example: Which body part is the odd one out—cornea, macula, lens, eyes, or iris? Really smart people seem to be saying, "The more you can see the pattern and your place in the pattern—where you fit and how things fit together—the more intelligent you are."

So how important is literal eyesight and figurative vision in your ability to be successful? Little Emmelyn Roettger's parents were told she might be autistic. It turned out she just needed glasses, and once they solved that problem she soon became the youngest US member of Mensa. And, by the way, the answer to the question above is: the eyes. The rest are all parts of the whole.

Just noticing the pattern, the way in which we are similar and are connected, can bring healing, strengthen the function of your brain, and help you to be more adaptable and intelligent. What do you see when you look at the people around you?

It is well into the twenty-first century, and there are still people who want me dead because I have the audacity to love a woman. For some people, that love is a serious lapse in judgment—a mistake that I should regret. But I do not repent the broken path that led me gaily forward to her.

Yes, I regret having an affair and hurting people along the way in my coming out process, starting with my parents. Imagine! There I was in Provo, Utah, a gift full of promise, a fifth-generation Mormon, born while my father served on a US naval ship in Japan.

Mormons, members of the Church of Jesus Christ of Latter-day Saints, believe that before birth, we lived with our heavenly father and mother. We had choices about the family, the community, and the country we were born into. Knowing what I know now, I would still choose the same amazing family and ascribe the same meaning to my life experiences.

In figuring out the pattern, I am constantly interpreting what I see and assigning it a meaning, a value. I think we all do this, though some of us might be more attuned to it than others. When my brother would take his three small boys to a store or a friend's house, he would walk in the door, look around, and say, "There! That chair is the time-out chair." His boys knew if they were good they could roam around, but if they were bad they would be sitting in that chair. The funny thing was, they might sit in any number of chairs in the course of an afternoon, but unless forced to they would never, ever sit in the time-out chair. My brother's words irrevocably changed the chair's meaning. Just his words had a powerful impact on a physical object and others' perception of it.

My parents are responsible for instilling a unique point of view in my siblings and me, I think. My father was an international businessman; my mother was an artist. Because of my family, "home" took on a series of unusual meanings. I know how small the world is and how deeply we are connected. I have seen beautiful patterns in the wings of a huge iridescent blue morpho butterfly, the Parisian night sky from the very top of the Eiffel Tower, a blue domed mosque on the Silk Road near the Afghan border, and a pride of lionfish in the Red Sea. Each image is a story without regrets.

When I was in my early twenties, I volunteered for the requisite year and a half of missionary service for the Mormon church and was called to the Tokyo North Mission. It was here that I learned the depth of my emotional strength, and did the hardest thing I have ever done: I shared what I believed deep down in my soul in an effort to bring people into my world and share the way I see our connection to the universe. I trained myself to be an extrovert, to talk to strangers to find where you and I can connect. I also learned Japanese, which meant I could do anything.

Once you see the big picture some things never feel like errors. As I kissed a girl during my junior year at Brigham Young University, I could almost hear outer voices cry, "Repent!" I felt compelled to keep it a shameful secret until I graduated in 1982, but I know now that my inner knowing was telling me all along that one thing leads to another, and now I am in the best relationship I can imagine. Most days I feel an overwhelming sense of gratitude for my experiences.

I do have some regrets, though. I regret allowing an ophthalmologist to predict my future when I was just twenty-eight years old. "Kimberly, you need to think about your life if you become blind. It is genetic, so there is nothing you can do." I wish I had said to him: "Bring it on! You have no idea who you're talking to. You have no idea about my drive, my curiosity, and my potential. You have no idea what might be discovered tomorrow that will change the face of genetic medicine forever or the healing potential of alternative medicine."

Instead of saying those things I just sat, stunned, and noticed the world suddenly seemed a little darker. My life as a professional photographer was already starting to slip away. But without that day I might not have gone to massage school, a profession where you don't necessarily need your sight, and I might not have gone on to study nutrition, acupressure, integrative manual therapy, or even the magical matrix energetics.

If I could travel back to that day in the ophthalmologist's office, I wouldn't change the trajectory that has created life-long learning and an amazing array of skills. Having walked a ways along the path of recovery, I can now reach out a helping hand to others, as I currently enjoy the best eyesight of my life. The brilliant physicist and inventor Albert Einstein said, "The most important decision we make is whether we believe we live in a friendly or hostile universe."

One of my clients put it this way: "I never wish bad things for people, but I am glad you almost went blind. You understand what I am saying, right?" I know she wishes me no harm. It is just that without experiencing that migraine pain, genetic eye dysfunction, and "impossible" diagnosis for myself, I might not be here supporting her recovery from the muscle weakness in her legs, and the fear driven deep into her heart by doctors predicting bad things for her future.

My biggest mistake was listening to the often well-meaning people who predicted negative outcomes, made assumptions about me and where I fit in, or assigned their own meaning to events and experiences in my life. But I have learned that since none of us can actually see the future, the smart choice is to predict a good one.

It is an interesting thing, our habit of making judgments without quite enough information. Lately, instead of trying to figure out what is good or evil, true or false, I try to see what is valuable. If it is useful, I employ it to improve the quality of my life, speed up healing in others, and help people feel stronger, move better, and contribute more fully to the community. I listen to other people's views on what I should or shouldn't do, but what I feel in the patterns and flow of my life matters the most. And I am grateful for *all* the pieces, regardless of how others may judge my life.

So in the end will my life be just a mix of accidental things that randomly happened? If so, I have been incredibly lucky. Perhaps fifty-five years ago, the universe and I planned out my life as part of some grand design. Perhaps I have experienced things so that I can creatively contribute in just the right way for you and for me.

Learn from other people. Absorb their wisdom and what is positive in what they offer. But above all, remember to believe in yourself.

The Call

ROSEMARY HURWITZ

Sometimes out of illness comes even greater health. This is the story of how I got well, and stayed that way.

When I was a college freshman, I suffered from acute clinical depression. In the midst of such darkness I couldn't see that my depression was a portal to my authentic self, a connection to Spirit. It would be many years before I would be able to fully process that. But my dark night of the soul gave me a strong foundation for a career in assisting others through their pain. Before I could help inspire others, though, I had to first do the hard work of telling the truth to myself.

I was a freshman at the local junior college and was having a difficult time sleeping or eating. After choking down my fears with a tasteless and little-eaten breakfast each morning,

I'd ride to school with my father who was a professor at a nearby Jesuit university.

I was not doing well in my science courses. In fact, I was having a hard time concentrating in any class, and it was taking a toll on my health and mental state.

My descent into depression aligned perfectly with the changing autumn weather. The piercing blue sky and fiery colored leaves were filled with the promise of all things dying. On this particular brilliant October morning I was feeling especially shaky, and I could not distract myself from the fears and panic anymore.

In class, every letter on the keyboard reminded me of something painful. Every part of me ached. And I lay my head on my arms, unable to move. I broke down right there.

Now, I see that I was losing the race against my higher self, who apparently needed to "enter" in just this way. Growth often feels like betrayal at first. But at the time I just felt alone.

The guidance counselor came to help me. She was an angel, gentle and kind, with a beautiful suit and perfectly manicured nails. We had a short talk in her office about how confused, scared, and lonely I felt. "I thought I wanted to be a nurse, but what am I doing?" I asked her.

She could see my deep exhaustion, and how my failure in class was just a symptom of something much larger going on, but she reassured me, saying that everything would work out for the best. She called my parents and my father said he was on his way. I sat there waiting with a heavy heart and a blank stare.

Soon I heard my father's voice, professorial and concerned, asking, "What seems to be the problem?"

"I don't know who I am," I whimpered.

"You are a child of God," he replied.

I managed to get six words to the surface: *"I don't know what that means."*

Deep down, I had really wanted to be at my father's university. Having a family member on faculty meant free tuition, and it was our only university option. But I was afraid to go there. My dad was a very strict disciplinarian, and I had witnessed his conflicts with my older sisters over their studies and social life. I had worked at a doctor's clinic during my last year of high school, and, wanting to make my own way, I made the decision to enroll in the junior college's nursing program. Now that I was failing my classes, I felt lost.

My father, loving and creative, but overbearing when stressed, took charge when we got home. "Something is deeply wrong," he told my mother. "She has not been well for over a month. We need to take her to a psychiatrist."

My mother, a Midwest farmer's daughter, was kind, peaceful, and a conflict avoider at all costs. She wanted to pray this away, but she reluctantly agreed. That night, relieved but shamed, I cried myself to sleep curled in the fetal position, only to wake drenched with fear.

||||||

My therapist's kind eyes were a soothing blue ocean. The moment he asked me, "Are you feeling a little confused?" I could feel a chunk of the burden I was carrying fall away. I shared my fears, told him I felt like I was going crazy. I was relieved when he said, "Crazy people usually don't realize they're crazy. No, you are just a little dependent and not liking yourself very much because of it. We will sort through it all."

The decision was made that I could benefit from inpatient treatment. But even with the medication they gave me, some days my anxiety brought me to such an intense place that I had to keep my hands busy just to feel some sense of the present moment. I made long scarves for my family and a needlepoint sampler that said "What We Are Is God's Gift to Us, What We *Become* Is Our Gift to God." I was literally knitting myself together.

I tried to settle in, but after seeing one mentally ill woman in the day room repeatedly shaking her crossed legs high into the air, and another patient talking to himself, I raced to my room. "Snap out of this!" I screamed at myself in the mirror. But I couldn't. I felt the stigma of the mentally ill.

Being hospitalized meant that I could not control my emotions or my state of mind, and I felt like a failure, or certainly a mistake. But the more the therapist and I talked about my family dynamics—my father's wild temper and controlling ways, my mother's acquiescence, and the expectation that we kids "honor thy mother and father" no matter what—the clearer it became that it was time for me to begin making my own decisions. With time, intense work, and sheer determination, I pushed through the darkness and began to learn about my strengths.

Over the course of three months in the hospital, I untangled my internalized rage at my parents and myself for our family's flaws. I realized that I was not the head of the family; I was the child looking for leadership. And I began to heal. Knowing that I was loved and that my parents did the best they could, I forgave them.

I came home but continued to go to therapy. At my mother's suggestion, I enrolled in modeling school, and soon professional modeling assignments came in regularly. My success gave me confidence, and after modeling for a year I decided to go to the university where my father taught. Once this door to myself opened wide, my commitment to my emotional and spiritual growth blossomed.

I forgave my father, but I knew I could never forget the patriarchal family dysfunction, for if I did I would be doomed to repeat it. Patriarchy was in steep decline on a societal level, too. It was the 1970s then, and the women's movement was surging. Like Maya Angelou, who as an abused child was mute but who ultimately found her voice, I was finding mine.

I finished college, found a wonderful career, and married the love of my life. My partner shared my vision for emotional health, and I felt happy and fulfilled. Through a program patterned after Marriage Encounter we became retreat facilitators for engaged couples. We practiced good communication and problem solving.

With the birth of each of our children I felt my intuition expand. This intuition helped me identify my deeper calling, and I completed a master's degree, which prepared me for the field of spiritual direction and education. I had never thought this would be a career I would pursue, but as John Lennon once wrote, "Life is what happens to you while you are busy making other plans."

One day while walking on campus I asked God, "How can I do this sacred work? I am just 'damaged goods' like everyone else." A soft but all-encompassing wind embraced me along with a deep inner knowing, and it said, "I will put the words inside your mouth."

As a wounded healer (way more healed than wounded now), I have trusted and followed that voice, doing adult spiritual education for ten years, coaching people for their own individuation and empowerment. Seeing the light in people's eyes as they realize their unique expression of the Divine, I feel a deep joy.

Being mistaken is *very different* from "being a mistake." I was mistaken in thinking that any of the dysfunction I experienced as a child was my fault, or that I was "damaged goods." I have now come full circle in my beliefs about that kind of pain and suffering.

What I have learned is that we all must experience hardship in some way if we are to experience true personal and spiritual growth—the ultimate abundance. Humility is a gift of humiliation, and we are all works in progress. "If God is before me, who can be against me?" I think.

What we see as failures or mistakes are often not so in the eyes of God. Rather, they are challenges for us to face, tests that we may even take on with the help of the Divine in order to grow, and in turn provide growth for the planet. We grow as individuals first, and then our strength ripples out to the people in our lives, and to the people in their lives, and the people in their lives, and on and on.

The path of our purpose is not always crystal clear, but it is always unfolding. Never lose sight of that. Wisdom has taught me that if you are patient and keep on, your purpose will manifest. Yours is already manifesting even if you can't see it just yet.

Breaking the Glass Ceiling

NANCY KAYE

It was the mid-1960s and I found myself a single mom of two small children, all alone and without a job. It was not my intention to be looking for work, or, for that matter, to be a single mom. But since my marriage had collapsed, I had no choice but to break out and find my own way in the world.

I had no idea how hard it would be. What was I qualified to do? Change diapers? Aside from being a nanny, I couldn't see a clear career path with my qualifications. My first passion had always been clothes (what young woman doesn't like fashion?), so I decided to try my hand in the fashion world. Being young and naïve, I assumed I could just walk into any women's clothing store in Los Angeles and get a job.

Family friends took pity on me and tried to jump-start my prospects on finding a job. They took me downtown to a headhunter who, after elaborating on my long list of accomplishments, laughed in my face. Apparently having the amazing ability to change a dirty diaper in under three minutes isn't highly sought after in the job market.

The headhunter stared at me until she realized that I had a family to support and I wasn't going away, and she had to do *something*. After much consternation, the headhunter found one opportunity for me—and I mean just one possibility—and it was up to me to get that position.

I interviewed with the junior and senior partners of a low-end maker of muumuu dresses designed for housewives who never had the need to take the curlers out of their hair. They offered me a sales position, and I gratefully took it knowing that I was the sole provider for my little family.

Unfortunately, I had no way of getting to my new job, so I was forced to borrow my ex-mother-in-law's car—a used Chevrolet Corvair. Each day I would commute for at least an hour through bumper-to-bumper freeway traffic, trekking from a small two-bedroom duplex in the Valley to downtown Watts, after attempting to get my children to their respective schools. My youngest, who was in preschool, refused to wear shoes and would take them off after I had put them on her three-year-old feet. And my oldest, who was in first grade, would cross her arms and refuse to get into the car. They would both cry and ask me why I had to go to work. I had no answer that their young minds would comprehend.

On my first day, I nodded as my boss told me that I needed to make appointments with buyers. He handed me a book and directed me to a closet-sized room with a phone and a chair. I closed the door and sat there wondering what and who a buyer was.

Knowing I had to figure this out quickly, I plowed through the book searching for understanding, and silently pleading for inner guidance. I stared at the list and hoped that my boss had not noticed the phone was not lit up while time slowly ticked by. Finally, I picked up the phone and made my first call.

I asked for the main buyer, not knowing his or her name, but hoping that the title would get me to a person. When I got my first buyer on the line, I was able to make an appointment to show her my company's line of low-end women's clothes. My first success!

As the day wore on, I made two more appointments for the very next day and my confidence was building. Despite the slow start, this job wasn't so difficult after all. As five o'clock approached, I closed the door to my closet, flung the bag of dresses over my shoulder, and headed home with a self-assured spring in my step.

The next day, after I fought to get my children off to school, fought the freeway traffic to work, and fought the desire to run and hide, I drove directly to my sales appointment. I parked, paid for parking, threw the garment bag over my shoulder, and went into the office for my first appointment with a satisfied stride. I had pumped myself up, ready to enter the appointment with courage, confidence, and a great smile. But my brief surge of dauntless exuberance was hopelessly dashed when the first buyer didn't even show up!

I drove to my second appointment, parked, and paid for parking. As I sat in the reception area, the buyer walked by me, telling the receptionist that she was leaving to go to the California Apparel Mart. I was stunned. Once again, I was being stood up. Unconsciously, I jumped up and introduced myself. I reminded her that we had an appointment, and she replied, "Reschedule," as she brushed me aside and walked out the door.

Dejected, I drove to my third appointment, put more money in the parking meter, and prayed that I would at least meet with the third buyer and that I would not return to my office empty-handed.

Her name was Shelly. There she was, honoring our appointment with a big, friendly, sweet smile. She had red hair and was exuberant. She surveyed my "lovely housewife dresses" with rapt attention, and bless her, she placed an order! My first order—thank you, Shelly! Thank you, universe!

With my first sale under my belt, the rest started to come more easily, and I settled into the routine of calling on buyers and adopting the fast pace of the industry. After a few years of working for that company, I decided it was time to up-level and get a higher-paying, more prestigious position to support my children and myself.

Was I scared by the prospect of further change? Sure I was. But the one thing the collapse of my marriage and forced entry into the job world had taught me was this: trust the universe. Through what had been the biggest unexpected change of my life, going from being a housewife and mother to a single parent and breadwinner, I learned that if I put my best foot forward, the universe would provide the rest.

With the power of trust at the forefront of my mind, I began the search for a new, better position. And within a week I received seven wonderful offers, each one better than the last.

I think it's important to point out that this was in the 1960s, and women were just emerging in the work force. There were even fewer women in upper management in the garment industry. I'm proud to report that I went on to become one of the first to change that, achieving the position of national sales manager, which had a salary that only 1 percent of American women had ever reached by that time.

None of this would have been possible without trust and hard work. When you are in those moments of dark despair, remember that the universe has a plan. But also remember that you can't sit around and wait for the universe to do the work as well—that part is up to you!

How to Tame a Ghost

NANCY SMITH

It was late morning, and I sat in the courthouse with my
Realtor and lawyer, about to purchase a beautiful house on the
water with a white picket fence. This was not the first time I
had been in this courthouse; years ago I was here when I lost
custody of my daughter and my son. The subsequent years
had been a rough road, but things were looking up.

The closing went well, and soon it was time to move in.
The house needed lots of work—paint, repairs, and lots of
love. The kitchen walls were blotches of three different col-
ors, the wainscoting was splashed with stains, and there was
mold. The countertop was made of broken tiles and wayward
glue that couldn't be wiped down. The living room was gray
with giant white stars and moons painted randomly on the
ceiling and the walls. In the basement was an assortment of

oddly shaped walls, complete with a door opening to nothing. None of this mattered to me, though. It was perfect because it was my home.

After a long day of homemaking, the temperature dropped suddenly at sunset, and I had to turn up the furnace. Around nine o'clock that night, *kaboom!* What sounded like a large explosion came from the basement, and I ran downstairs to see what had happened. But everything was fine—the furnace was humming, nothing was out of place. I was rattled by not having found the reason for the noise, but I went back upstairs and continued working.

That night, as I went to bed, I was unnerved and feeling out of sorts. I woke up with a start shortly after I fell asleep. Something had happened in the house. I had an eerie feeling of being watched.

Let me back up here for a second. I am a practicing medium, and a while back I'd sat in a medium's circle and received a message that I would move into a house on the water with a white picket fence. At the time I was penniless and couldn't imagine that message was for me. But I made a deal with myself: when I got back on my feet I would make some changes.

Shortly after that reading I was offered a job that changed everything. Financial security, a salaried position with insurance, and benefits and a savings program! And now, a little over a year later, there I was.

I was used to spirits being around me, but this was something very different. I walked through the house and saw that my favorite clock had fallen off the wall and smashed to pieces. Shuddering, I walked back upstairs and tucked myself into bed, certain that morning couldn't come soon enough. "Scaredy-cat," I muttered to myself. I called in my angels and protectors to surround me and protect and comfort me.

The next morning I called a plumber and had him come over to look at the furnace, explaining the coldness in the evenings and the loud bang. He couldn't find anything wrong, but he tuned up the furnace and put in a new thermostat to mollify me. That night was the same as before: the cold, the explosion, the foreboding.

During my evening meditation I asked my spirit animal to sit at the end of my bed to help me feel safe. I have a totem animal guide, a wolf, whom I became aware of when my children were preschoolers. I often saw him out of the corner of my eye, always ready to give me a heads up or reassure me when I felt anxious. He was big and shaggy, with dark fur, large, loving eyes, and a calm nature. He showed up now in the house to help me through this one.

I asked him to work with me to understand why I felt so anxious. Had I made a mistake in choosing this house? Was it me, was I suffering from some kind of post-traumatic anxiety? I couldn't hear a clear answer, but I had to trust that it would show up. Turning this *Titanic* around was going to take time.

It wasn't long before I met my new neighbor, Tom. He welcomed me to the neighborhood and was thrilled to tell me about my house. Apparently, the previous owner's husband had had a bad temper and was very moody, and she eventually threw him out. A few years later, she took her husband Carlos back during his final stages of lung cancer. He was miserable. He was on oxygen and spent most of his time in a little room off the kitchen. He still smoked. One day his cigarette lit his oxygen on fire. The whole room exploded, and he inhaled the flames. He died shortly after being rushed to the hospital.

That night, I asked my wolf about what Tom had told me. As I meditated I realized that I was living with a spirit who had a very similar profile to my ex-husband. Wonderful. How was I to work with this new information?

I awoke in the middle of the night struggling to breathe. It felt like there were hands on my throat and I was choking. Just as I woke up, I caught a glimpse of a man in a white shirt standing in my bedroom doorway. I froze with fear. Where were my helpers, my guides and protectors? How did this energy get through to me? I did relaxation exercises and soothing mental meditations to calm myself down. I wrapped myself in my warmest blankets. As my cold body warmed up I began to relax, and sleep took me.

Suddenly, the long fangs of a wolf flashed in my face and lunged toward my throat. I reacted quickly, wrapping my legs around his body and my hands around his neck, pushing his head away from mine. Adrenaline pumped through me and replaced the paralyzing fear I had been in. As I fought, anger welled up in me and overflowed. Then rage took over, and I fought as I had never fought before. I would not stop.

I kept fighting until the wolf began to pull away, and then I attacked, wanting to beat this vicious animal into a pulp. He finally lay there, nearly dead, and I kicked him, wanting to finish the job. He raised his head, looking at me, and said, "You need to start fighting."

I woke up in a sweat, shaking and panting. What the hell was that? *Start fighting?* What did that mean? What had I been doing all these years if not fighting? To survive my ex's attacks I'd *had* to fight. I fought hard to actually have a life after years of living in fear of an angry husband. I thought about how I managed to get back up from the falls, how I learned to trust my own resources and myself, and then I realized that the ghost in the house was showing me where I still needed to heal, where I still needed to grow.

By noon the next day, I had a plan. I went to the hardware store and picked up a soothing color of paint. I shopped around at the thrift store and found some beautiful mirrors and a rug trimmed in blood red. For the next few nights I worked on that little room off the kitchen. I sanded and primed the trim and the walls and painted them a new color. I hung the curtains and rolled out the rug. I hung pictures on the wall and gave them each a shot of Reiki so they would stay up. Then I set up the healing table and a set of shelves that held my music and books and crystals I had finally unpacked. Perfect. The room glowed. The energy was shifting.

I cast a circle with Spirit and breathed intentions into the walls, the windows, and the floor that claimed only love, peace, and calm could exist in the room. Then I extended the circle to encompass the entire house and yard. I called in the spirit Carlos and invited him to participate in this place of healing. I claimed healing for myself and healing for Carlos.

Eventually I looked at the clock. It was after ten. Where was my explosion? I was warm as toast and felt very peaceful.

My life had been completely undone through a bad marriage and an even worse divorce. As I tried to piece my life back together I found I was only able to do it on a superficial level. I had finally reached a financial milestone in my life when I was able to buy a house for myself, to replace the house I had lost. Once I moved in and began to settle myself, I soon experienced the same fear and anxiety I had experienced in my marriage—only this time it was a ghost wreaking havoc in my home.

The energy shifted within me as I dug into my deepest hidden fears and owned these realizations, and everything else shifted with it. I realized a deep inner healing for myself and changed my environment when I acknowledged and embraced myself completely.

Through this experience I learned the importance of accepting ourselves in all our darkness and vulnerability as well as our strength and vision. When we deny our own secret dark truths, they will haunt us and disrupt us, even when we think we are at our strongest capacity. But when we choose to do our healing work, our lives will change!

There had been two ghosts in this house—and one of them had been me. Thankfully, the *Titanic* had just turned around.

Breaking Down
and Breaking Through

CHRISTIE MELONSON

I looked in the mirror and realized for the first time that I couldn't recognize my own face. The voice inside me screamed: "I don't know who I am anymore!" The realization sent shock waves through my body. I couldn't believe my life had come to such an extraordinarily low point.

After days of crying, sitting in a dark room with the shades drawn, sleeping fitfully, and enduring intense stomachaches, I realized that I was not a confident, liberated, professional woman who had traveled the world and educated herself. I had lied to myself about who I was. I pretended that everything was OK when it was not. I knew in that moment that I had been unconsciously following the patterns of society, especially the messages about how women are not important without their male counterparts.

I suddenly became aware that it was time to take off the mask and unveil the truth to myself about the person I'd unconsciously transformed into over the years. It finally hit me that I was in an abusive relationship. I knew that I was unhappy, and if I let this unholy alliance continue, the death of my physical body or spirit would soon follow. In fact, I already felt like a wilting flower, and I was losing strength every day.

The end of that era still remains hazy in my mind, which is hardwired very differently today. The moment I thought I was going to lose my life this handsome man, with his charming smile and his magical way with people, gently looked me in my eyes and without hesitation reached out and began choking me.

Of course, in that instant I couldn't believe it was happening. I couldn't move, I couldn't fight, and I couldn't speak. I stood paralyzed for what seemed like an eternity and then prayed to God to help me. I then felt a warm, bright light around my solar plexus and heard the voice of my guardian angel who told me exactly what to say and gave me the strength to mutter a few words. Upon whispering the magical words, the man who had my life in his hands in so many ways let me go.

While it may not sound like a miracle to most, I can now see that incident was a physical manifestation of what was already happening to me emotionally in that relationship. I was being smothered by the weight of my own anxiety and humiliation. All of the years of insults, maltreatment, and lies had finally manifested into the physical world. I had learned to hate myself. All the hate cast on me started to flow through my veins as if it were part of me. Ironically, it was during the struggle for my life that I realized that I was of value, made in the image of God. At that point I started to live my life with dignity.

The man whom I loved totally and faithfully was clearly not on my side and could no longer remain in my life. I could see that I had been spiritually poisoned for a long time with self-doubt, and that my mind began to play tricks on me about what I was truly capable of achieving, and what type of life I knew I truly deserved.

Unfortunately, my boyfriend refused to let go without a fight, and he continued to beg relentlessly for me to give him another chance. After days of stalling I made the bold move to let him into my home; not for the purpose of reconciling the relationship, but to confront him for the last time.

Despite the previous incident, I wasn't afraid. Rather, I was resigned to the fact that if I were to truly heal someday, I could never win the game of life by using the tactics of an oppressor. Instead of fighting, I decided to make a declaration. I looked him in his eyes and told him: "You can never kill my spirit. I'm like one of those little plants growing up from underneath the sidewalk." I remember the look of shock on his face and the surge of energy and light that flooded my entire being in that moment. I knew I was done, and he knew it, too.

But my work had just begun, as my metamorphosis required a shift in my relationship with myself. I realized once and for all that I needed to learn how to love myself with all my imperfections. After all, the only way I was going to be safe was to choose to live a life of freedom from that point on; for me that meant no longer putting up with abuse. I couldn't afford to be a prisoner of someone else's desires or unrealistic standards for perfection.

Facing the challenge head-on, I began getting to know myself better, taking myself out on dates, and breaking out of my shell. I declared my devotion to my relationship with myself to everyone and aired secrets about the past. People were shocked. They never imagined what I had been through. I volunteered at a shelter for women and children who had been through domestic violence to remind me of where I could have ended up. I sought to redefine myself by what I gave to this world through renewing my spiritual practices and increasing my charity toward others.

Maya Angelou said it best: "When someone shows you who they are, believe them the first time." I say if folks mistreat you, bless them and set them free! Of course, this is hard to do when we are afraid of being alone, or we doubt our own self-worth. However, when we have the inner confidence to face the risk of uncertainty associated with being single, and cling to the faith that we are on earth for a purpose, there is always the possibility that we will meet loving companions as we continue along our path. And even if we don't, with a healthy sense of self-love, we can endure moments of being single with peace, happiness, and joy—even when society tells us that we should not feel whole.

My life today is a completely different story than it was all those years ago. With a healthy sense of self, I have pursued many of my professional goals and discovered that I had talents I never previously imagined—namely, the ability to assist people in their own healing journeys, to teach, and to write, to name a few. My life philosophy has also changed tremendously. Instead of seeing life as a fight for survival, I see it as an opportunity to nourish and grow the talents in others.

It's often said that the world is your mirror; that we see on the outside that which is truly inside of us. I once saw darkness because I was drowning in negativity and humiliation. Now, years later, I have watched the sunrise in my soul, and I can see the beauty in others and in life. My hope is that anyone who has survived an abusive relationship will join me on the brighter side of life, in a brilliant world full of healing and serenity and possibilities, where you don't have to mask who you are, where you have a voice, and where you can breathe freely. When I look in the mirror now, I don't see someone who is perfect, but someone who is real and honest and happy.

Calm and Connected
in the Midst of Life's Travails

KATHY JACKSON

It was Monday, January 2, 2012, when I loaded the truck and headed to Beaver, Oklahoma. A snowstorm was forecasted for the panhandle so I decided to leave before the storm blew in. Normally I would take Zeus, my trusted canine companion, but the hotels did not accept animals. The decision to leave him safely at home with the warmth of a heated 8' x 10' doghouse seemed like the logical choice.

When I returned on Wednesday evening it was rather peculiar that the dogs greeted me as I parked in the driveway, given that I had securely locked all the gates. Fortunately, all of the dogs were there—except for Zeus! Immediately I started searching for him everywhere I could think of: in the pasture, down the road, and even at the neighbors'.

To confuse matters more, I could not figure out how the dogs had gotten out. All of the gates were locked just as they were when I left; everything appeared to be in order. Then I saw it. Somebody had cut the fence! Zeus had been stolen!

Now other things started to make sense. I thought of that blue car with the plastic covering the passenger side rear window that had passed by the house several times a day for the last week. My initial suspicion had been that the two men in it were casing the house for a robbery. Instead, they had wanted my dog. My heart sank. At the time I did not understand why anyone would come out to the middle of nowhere to take a beautiful, ninety-pound, barrel-chested, brindle boxer.

But at that moment the why didn't matter; my job now was to find Zeus and bring him home safely. I hung flyers. I asked the neighbors. I stopped people on the streets. I talked to the police and visited local veterinarians. I did everything imaginable to cover as wide an area as possible.

I was incredibly upset when none of these activities produced any results, but I knew in my heart that I had to stay calm and get silent for a positive outcome. I called my friend Joannara, who is an animal communicator. She explained to me what was necessary for Zeus's safe return: nonstop heart energy. I had to connect a highway of love and light between the two of us. Zeus needed an "energetic map" in order to find his way home.

On my way home from another round of searching, I traveled past a local gas station. It's a friendly place, right on the outskirts of town. Something told me to stop and put up a flyer. I learned a long time ago to trust those feelings.

It was Sunday evening when my phone rang and a woman introduced herself as Hollie. She told me she saw the flyer at the gas station and recognized Zeus as a stray that had been wandering in her neighborhood. Talk about jubilation! I was jumping up and down with excitement.

Foxy, my miniature Australian shepherd, and I quickly loaded into the truck and went to Hollie's neighborhood. We searched and called for hours, but there was no sign of Zeus. Once, Foxy even picked up Zeus's scent and carefully placed a few of her own, but we couldn't find him. We returned home disappointed, but hopeful and also grateful he had managed to escape from his abductees.

The next morning we loaded into the truck again, drove to the neighborhood, and stopped to listen. I connected my energies with Zeus and asked him to guide me to him. We started down a dirt road that ran alongside Hollie's house. It also ran, according to the map, perpendicular to the road in front of my house. It was at least ten miles before the roads would intersect, but I felt energetically that this was the direction Zeus had gone.

As we headed back to the truck, there was a herd of cows led by a bull that came up over a rise, walking single file. They walked over to the fence near the road.

Looking at the bull, it was as if he said to me, "You're the one lookin' for that city dog?"

"Yep," I replied.

"He went up the road. Headed home."

I thanked them and turned toward the truck. One of the cows started to call out at the top of her lungs as though she were calling to Zeus to let him know we were there. Then the entire herd turned and walked back over the rise and out of sight.

When we drove to where the roads intersected, Foxy jumped out of the truck even before I could come to a full stop. She ran around the house on the corner sniffing like there was no tomorrow. Zeus had been here. I could feel it, and so could Foxy. We searched around there for hours, but still no Zeus.

The next morning I needed an emotional break, so I headed to the city to meet my sister and her boys for lunch. When my phone rang, it was my neighbor.

"My sister swears this is your dog," said the friendly voice on the line. "He showed up yesterday, came inside last night, and lay down on the floor like he was home. I put him out in the barn for the night."

My heart raced and my breath caught in my stomach. Could it really be that Zeus would soon be home, safe and sound? I raced to my neighbor's house and was thrilled to find Zeus sleeping in the front yard. Thank God, Zeus was safe!

I knew then that it wasn't only our relentless searching and prayers that brought Zeus home. It was the pure spiritual connection between humans and animals. As an animal lover, I had always felt this connection—but that day when

I saw Zeus snoozing peacefully in the yard, I realized that by staying calm and connected to the source, and by following the guidance that is given, we can create miracles in our own lives.

When unexpected things happen in life, the most important teaching I can share with you is this: stay calm, stay connected to the source, and listen to the guidance. Zeus returning home after being stolen was a true miracle. I believe there is a spiritual connection between humans and animals. Next to Spirit, this connection is the purest of them all.

Reset Your Life!

||||||||||||||||||||||||||||||||||||||||||||||||||||||||||||||||||||||||||||||||||||||||||||||||||||||||||||||||||

VICKI HIGGINS

||||||||||||||||||||||||||||||||||||||||||||||||||||||||||||||||||||||||||||||||||||||||||||||||||||||||||||||||||

Hi there, I'm Vicki. I'm eight and a half years old. I live in Indiana with my mom, dad, and little sister. My dad is a supercool race car driver. My mom is the most awesome mom on the block, and she stays home with us—so fun! I feel like a princess and I even live in a castle with a moat! I hope I get a pony for Christmas!!!

||||||||

Hey, I'm twelve years old and I've started to figure a few things out. Like, I really don't live in a castle. I live in a small ranch-style home where things don't work and they don't get fixed. That moat I mentioned? It was really just a flooded basement, a waterproofing project gone wrong. Yet another one of my dad's failed attempts at home improvement just to save a dime. Oh, and I figured out that my dad isn't a cool Indy car driver, he's just a pissed-off truck driver who still dreams of racing, which I know will *never* happen. I love my mom—she's awesome—but now she can't stay home with us because someone has to pay the bills, so she's gone a lot. What do I want for Christmas? Well, I just hope we get a few presents and maybe Dad will be on the road!

|||||||

What's up? I'm fourteen now. I don't care about ponies, Christmas, or much else right now—except for getting the hell out of here! Dad's lost it—I mean really lost it! Last night he threw a couch at me. I'm not kidding, a couch. Just because I came home late from my *second* job of the day. Yes, I work at a bakery before school, go to school all day, and then I babysit for the neighbors after school. Not only did my loser dad throw a couch at me, but he also decided to hit me with his belt again. It wasn't the first time, but it's the last. I will never be like that, and I am definitely changing my life no matter what it takes.

I woke up this morning and my dad was gone. Mom says for good. I hope so. Hey, you know what? It kinda feels like Christmas.

|||||||

Thanks for reading a little bit of my story. I know I'm not the only person who's lived through tough times. I know that you, like me, have experienced your fair share of dreams, hopes, and disappointments. But I also know—because you are reading this—that you are committed to creating your best life. And I can help. I'll share with you how I pushed the reset button on my life and take you through the steps so that you can too. I want you to know that you can start fresh no matter where you're at today.

Why should you trust me to help you? Well, like you, I've been in some pretty tough spots in the past. I grew up with a bipolar father, and I endured physical and verbal abuse, which resulted in extreme shyness, limited belief in myself, and poor choices. I also went through a number of ups and downs. I was the victim of an attempted abduction, and then later I went through a painful divorce and debilitating depression.

Growing up in an abusive home was no doubt detrimental to my well-being. But it taught me unwavering drive and the tenacity to create a better life for myself. I believe that where there is a will there is a way, no matter what your background or circumstances. And now, I'm a self-made, pull-myself-up-by-my-bootstraps professional.

I worked hard through high school and college, putting myself through school by working two jobs. I earned my undergrad degree in sports marketing and exercise physiology and then went on to earn my MBA. I knocked on a lot of doors to break into the world of business those first couple years out of college, and I think my toughness growing up helped me to be fearless as I ventured out to begin my career. That drive and hard work got me into some pretty great places:

- I had a ten-year career with the Indiana Pacers (in the Reggie Miller days).
- I worked with ATA Airlines in marketing the major events of the NBA, MLB, and NFL across the United States.
- Working with the Los Angeles Tourism Board, I helped market LA to the world.
- I'm now the executive vice president and chief marketing officer for Visit Newport Beach (a.k.a. paradise), and I also teach marketing through Destination Marketing Association International.

I've been to every major city in the United States and watched most major sporting events from the field—all-star games, playoff games—and I've been to twenty-seven Indy 500 races. I've attended the Grammys, the Emmys, the Academy Awards, and the Cannes Film Festival. I've been to Australia, where I biked wine country, saw my first kangaroo, and went paddleboarding at Bondi Beach. The executives of Harrods of London gave me an insider's tour of London. Oh, and I rappelled off a thirty-two-story hotel in LA for charity.

I've been where you've been, and that includes some pretty tough spots. But I've also been where you want to go—some pretty cool places! And I know that if I can do it, you can too.

Of course a lot of people have hope for a better life, but they don't have a plan to make it a reality, and without a plan it's easy to fall back into old habits and limiting beliefs. The process I call Resetting Your Life is kind of like creating a roadmap to fulfill your dreams. It doesn't matter what kind of life you dream of—business owner, yoga teacher, race car driver, or just the ability to be happy every day—all you need is hope and hard work! Oh yes, and a *strategy.*

I will share with you my five-step strategy that can work for anyone who is willing to apply it. By following these simple steps, you can let go of your past stories, overcome challenges, and go forward to create your best life.

To begin, I'm going to ask you a series of questions. And here's the important part: to receive the full benefit of this exercise, I need you to write down your answers. These answers are for your eyes only, but please trust me on this point, as I can assure you that part of the magic occurs when you put these answers on paper. By writing these things down, you will be able to see patterns in your life that you may otherwise miss, and you will be signaling to yourself and the universe that you are serious about change.

Now let's dig in by tapping in to your creative energy, your inner spirit, and your unique potential.

1. *Set the foundation.* Consider your past. What were the biggest challenges in your life that you have had to overcome? What accomplishments or events are you most proud of? It is important to take an honest look at where you are in your life, and how you got there.

2. *Find the gold.* What were the gifts that came because of those major challenges? Ironically, I believe that our biggest challenges in life often produce the greatest gifts. We have to go through these events in order to learn things about ourselves, or to be able to help others going through similar situations. What did you gain or learn as a result of your major challenges? And let's not forget about your accomplishments and positive events too—what did you gain or learn from them?

3. *Write out your dream life.* Dream big here! Now that you know where you have been, let's see where you want to go! What would your perfect life consist of? I use a system of "the 8 *F*s" to help me account for all of the important categories in my life.

    •   *Faith:* What would your spiritual life be? Are you religious? Are you spiritual? Are you taking time to connect to your higher power or to your spiritual guides? Does this involve more prayer or meditation? Or a trip to the great outdoors? How can you further enhance this connection? Be specific.

    •   *Family:* What would the relationships be like with your spouse, your children, your parents, your siblings, and other relatives? Take time and write down each person and what your dream life would be like as it relates to them and how you want to feel around them.

    •   *Friends:* What would your friendships be like? Would you have more quality friendships and fewer friends of convenience? How would you feel around your friends? List the things you would have in common with your ideal friends, as well as the qualities they would posses, like honesty, self respect, etc. What types of people do you want to surround yourself with?

- *Fitness:* Would you like to have more energy and vitality throughout your day? What can help you get there? Yoga? Exercise? What type of physical activities would you like to do? What types of foods would fuel your body and help it be the healthiest it can be?

- *Fun:* What do you consider fun? This is just you—what makes you smile and laugh? What are your secret pleasures? What fun things would be involved in your perfect life? Remember not to judge here, just list what sounds fun to you!

- *Firm:* What would your ideal career be? If you could get paid for doing something you love, what would you do all day? And don't forget, running a household is one of the most difficult jobs of all. How would your household run in this ideal scenario?

- *Finances:* What would your financial situation look like? How much would you have in savings? How much would you make each month? How much would you have for fun money each month?

- *Feelings:* How would you feel? List the feeling words that describe how you want to feel in your life: peaceful, happy, grateful, energized, etc.

4. *Create your strategy.* What are a few steps that you could take in each of your 8 *F*s to get you closer to your goal in each of those areas? Be specific here. Write down just

one or two steps that would move the needle in each area. Be sure to keep these ideas focused on things that you have control of—your actions, your attitude, things that you can physically *do* to move things forward.

5. *Make a plan for action and execute.* Now that you've written down where you have been, what you gained from it, where you want to go, and what you need to do to get there, it's time to create a specific plan for when and how you will take action on the steps listed in your strategy. Make an action plan for this week, this month, and even this year, listing the specific actions you will take and when you will take them. Keep this list and check the items off as you go. If you have to change a date or alter a plan, that's OK, just remember to keep your eye on the prize of resetting your life.

OK, I know this sounds like a lot all at once. But remember you don't have to *do* it all at once. The key here is to remember that getting where you want to go takes effort and consistency. Baby steps are okay. Just remember to stick to your plan and move forward.

Now you are ready to begin walking—or maybe running—down the path to your own successful future. You *can* make your world better. It just takes a new perspective. You are the one in control of your life. You are the one who takes the action steps to create new outcomes.

There was a time when if you had told me I'd one day be scuba diving in the Caribbean on a private yacht, or that I'd meet Richard Branson, I would have told you no way. But who knows where I'd be today if I'd had a cakewalk of an upbringing. The challenges I dealt with growing up actually allowed me to envision a future where I wouldn't be burdened with hardship and pain. And once I had the ability to actually do something about it, I made sure to seize the opportunity to do as much as I can in this short life. Bad luck, bad circumstances, even bad people, are not in our lives permanently. There is very little that is permanent, actually. And you have the power to contribute positively to the world around you, create the life you *want* to live, and be who you are meant to be.

I'd like to leave you with one of my favorite quotes from Howard Thurman:

Don't ask yourself what the world needs. Ask yourself what makes you come alive and then go do that. Because what the world needs is people who have come alive.

You have the responsibility, and the opportunity, to overcome challenges and change your life, and create for yourself and your family the life you desire. Before you know it, you will be doing what you are meant to do, loving your life, and making a difference for yourself, your family, and the planet! The world is waiting for you to come alive.

Author Biographies

Madisyn Taylor

Best-selling author Madisyn Taylor is the co-founder and editor in chief of the popular inspirational website DailyOM (www.dailyom.com). A recognized leader in self-help and New Thought spirituality, she has more than fifteen years of experience in personal development and alternative-healing methodologies. When not working, Madisyn can be found meditating in her garden and communing with nature. She lives in Ojai, California, with her husband, Scott Blum, and their son, Oliver.

Sunny Dawn Johnston

Sunny Dawn Johnston is a gentle, loving, and supportive inspirational teacher, author, motivational speaker, and psychic medium. She has helped thousands of people across the country find their personal spiritual connection, recognize and "own" their natural spiritual gifts, and listen to their inner truth. Sunny is the founder of Sunlight Alliance LLC, a spiritual teaching and healing center in Glendale, Arizona. She also volunteers her time as a psychic investigator for the international organization FIND ME. She is the author of *Invoking the Archangels: A Nine-Step Process to Heal Your Body, Mind, and Soul.*

You can learn more about Sunny by visiting her website at: www.sunnydawnjohnston.com.

HeatherAsh Amara

HeatherAsh Amara is the founder of TOCI—the Toltec Center of Creative Intent, based in Austin, Texas—which fosters local and global community that supports authenticity, awareness, and awakening. She is dedicated to inspiring depth, creativity, and joy by sharing the most potent tools from a variety of world traditions. HeatherAsh studied and taught extensively with don Miguel Ruiz, author of *The Four Agreements,* and continues to teach with the Ruiz family. She is the author of *The Toltec Path of Transformation: Embracing the Four Elements of Change, Sacred Time Management,* and *Toltec Tarot.*

Tenaya Asan

From early on in childhood, Tenaya has been passionate about well-being: individual, collective, and planetary. Through many years of dedication to her own personal growth, Tenaya knows what it takes to overcome destructive behavior patterns consequential to a traumatic childhood in order to live and share her passion. She is a liscensed teacher of *The Art of Feminine Presences,* teaches her own workshop, *Our Souls Reunion* "Coming Home to Ourselves and One Another,"and is a personal coach. You can find additional information about Tenaya and the work she does at: www.tenayaasan.com.

Robyn Benson, DOM

A graduate of the University of Virginia with a bachelor of science degree in sports medicine, Robyn began studying Chinese medicine in 1989. With twenty years of professional experience, she specializes in pain management, women's health, herbal medicine, IV therapies, cutting-edge energy medicine, and family medicine. A knowledgeable acupuncturist and herbalist, Dr. Benson is board-certified in orthopedic and pediatric acupuncture and practices many forms of alternative, progressive internal, and preventive medicines. She is the founder of Santa Fe Soul Health and Healing Center, the Santa Fe Soul Foundation, and, most recently, the Self-Care Revolution movement with a mission to change the face of healthcare. Dr. Benson is married and has two children, Harrison and Hannah. She is a marathon runner, world traveler, public speaker, and activist for social change.

Mandy Berlin

Mandy Berlin, MEd, is an author, teacher, intuitive counselor, and retired statistician. She successfully completed her doctoral comprehensive examinations in educational psychology at Arizona State University. Her harrowing journal, *Death Is Not "The End": One Agnostic's Journey on the Bumpy Road to Belief,* describes the traumatic yet awe-inspiring transformation she experienced following the death of her husband and a number of friends and loved ones. For the past six years, Ms. Berlin has been applying the Law of Attraction to her life, while instructing friends and relatives in the attraction process. Visit her blog: http://mandymax .blogspot.com or website: http://www.worldwidewhoswhoreleases .com/press-release/mandy-berlin-med-recognized-by-worldwide -whos-who.

Kimberly Burnham

Kimberly Burnham, PhD, known as "The Nerve Whisperer," helps visionaries improve their eyesight, insights, confidence, and brain health. Backed up by a PhD in integrative medicine, her childhood as a global nomad, and her own vision recovery, Kim is passionate about helping people see and feel seen. She works toward healing social issues like bullying and global statistics like 2,000 suicides a day, as well as creating food sustainability in partnership with organizations like Hazon, which means "vision" in Hebrew. See Kim and read her other published work at: www.kimberlyburnham.com.

Patricia Cohen

Patricia Cohen currently sits on the board of Nevada County Public Television Station NCTV 11. She is a former president of the board of the Nevada County Jewish Community Center, vice president of the board of the Mariposa Waldorf School, and vice president of the board and program coordinator of New Frontiers of the Gold Country, a nonprofit educational organization. Her education in human development and work with children in religious schools, public schools, day care centers, and juvenile halls have given her a unique insight into the benefit of ritual and tradition as a tool for the unification of families.

In her book *The Sacred American,* Patricia ventures beyond the mundane drudgery of day-to-day survival by offering meaningful solutions to the challenges of our time. Visit her website at: www .sacredamerican.com.

Siobhan Coulter

Siobhan Coulter is an Australian psychologist, light worker, and author. She believes in living a life grounded in unconditional love and being fully connected to her light. Siobhan supports others in doing the same by helping them clear their karma and encouraging them to create a life that is complete, joyous, and free. This is her second published work. Her first chapter, "Just Being You: The Secret to Inner Bliss" was published in *Pearls of Wisdom: 30 Inspirational Ideas to Live Your Best Life Now!*

Follow Siobhan on Facebook at: www.facebook.com/siobhan coulter1 and visit her website, www.siobhancoulter.com.

Carol J. Craig

Carol J. Craig is an expatriate who teaches overseas. She has worked in Port of Spain; Trinidad; Cairo, Egypt; and in Nairobi, Kenya, in private national schools as a secondary science teacher. Prior to teaching, Carol worked in retail management in Arizona and Nevada and also for the US government in Colorado. She has a bachelor's degree in forestry resource management with an emphasis in business and a master's degree in education with a focus on biology. Carol continues to teach and never knows where she and her husband will be headed next. She enjoys having an unknown future, thrives on change, and loves the adventures that living overseas provides.

Karen Curry

Karen Curry is the author of the upcoming book *Understanding Human Design: The New Science of Astrology* (Hierophant Publishing, September 2013). Over the past ten years as a human design student and teacher, Karen has facilitated hundreds of readings and taught more than a thousand hours of teleclasses, workshops, and webinars. She is the founder of the Human Design for Everyone Training Program and has trained more than five hundred people to use human design as part of their life-coaching and healing practices.

Anne M. Deatly

Anne M. Deatly, PhD, is a former principal research scientist in vaccine research at Pfizer. She is now an Eden Energy Medicine Certified Practitioner, teacher, and inspirational speaker. As director of the Optimal Health and Wellness Center (www.energizeforjoy .com), she focuses on holistic health and energy balancing, positive inspiration, and spiritual coaching. Her goal is to show people how to revitalize their life and radiate joy. Known as the Radiant Energy Doctor, Anne is a radio talk show host of *Energy Medicine and Optimal Health* on VoiceAmerica's Health and Wellness channel. Anne was selected as one of the original messengers at the Messenger Summit in San Diego, March and October 2012.

Karen Hasselo

Karen Hasselo is an LCSW who will soon complete her certification for spiritual life coaching through Holistic Learning Centers (HLC) of New Jersey. She is also training to become an instructor with HLC. Karen resides with her special-needs son in Naperville, Illinois, and can be reached at: kahass22@gmail.com.

Vicki Higgins

Vicki Higgins serves as the executive vice president and chief marketing officer for Newport Beach & Co., the official marketing organization for the City of Newport Beach, California. She leads a team of professionals to execute cutting-edge marketing efforts to create awareness and drive business. Vicki is passionate about professional and personal growth. She is a sought-after speaker, sharing her story of overcoming challenge to inspire people to create their best life.

Rosemary Hurwitz

Rosemary Hurwitz has a communications degree from Marquette University and a master of arts in pastoral studies from Loyola University of Chicago.

She has more than twenty years of experience in career consulting, and, along with her husband, Rosemary facilitated retreats for Discovery, a program for engaged couples patterned after Marriage Encounter.

Committed to self-awareness as well as personal and spiritual growth, her presentations, workshops, and individual sessions focus on wellness through the Enneagram. The Enneagram is a time-honored system for understanding the nine universal personality types and living from the higher authentic self.

Visit Rosemary at: www.spiritdrivenliving.com and on Facebook at: www.facebook.com/spiritdrivenliving.

Kathy Jackson

Kathy Jackson holds a bachelor's degree in accounting from Oklahoma State University and is co-owner of Wind Gear, Inc. Her spiritual quest began November 2, 1989, the day of her grandfather's funeral, when at the age of twenty-five she asked a question of him: "What am I supposed to do with my life?" The answer would prove to be the map that has transformed her life. Kathy was born and raised in Oklahoma, the sixth of seven children, and blessed by loving and wonderful parents, Jim and Shirley Jackson.

Sara Jane

Sara Jane is the founder of the Healing Energy of Sound, a technique that uses toning from the voice to empower an individual's own self-healing. Sara has spoken and given demonstrations at events in the United Kingdom and the United States, sharing the power of this modality.

She is also a Reiki master teacher and practitioner and acts as a channel for the wisdom of the realms.

Sara draws on her own life experiences and healing journey to support those who attend her courses and workshops.

For more information about Sara and her work see her website, www.thespiritof-love.com.

Nancy Kaye

Nancy is a former TV and radio host, author, and speaker. Her written work has appeared in 122 countries, and she has interviewed many famous people, including His Holiness the Dalai Lama, Dr. Deepak Chopra, Dr. Wayne Dyer, and more. As founder of the Confident Communicator™ Workshops, Nancy instructs one-on-one personalized and group training reprogramming sessions globally in all areas of communication. The intensive curriculum is tailored to the needs of each client. She diagnoses, evaluates, and teaches clients, offering coaching, on-call client support, and empowerment.

She is also the founder of Define Your Destiny™ Intensives, a unique self-development intensive that gives clients powerful tools to use and build on to discover and live their perfect life plan (www.defineyourdestiny.com), and she is a contributing editor at *Integral Yoga Magazine,* where she heads the West Coast bureau office.

Christine Krinke, PhD

Christine Krinke, PhD, is the founder of Light Alliance, a Holistic Institute for Research and Development. She became interested in the alternative healing arts after a near-death experience more than twenty years ago. She holds a PhD in metaphysics and is an intuitive, Seichim Reiki master teacher, certified transpersonal hypnotherapist, motivational speaker, writer, teacher, and trainer. Chris has been a guest on many radio shows, and her work has been featured in several magazines. Chris travels extensively, speaking at expos around the country. Her training and experiences have taught her how to help people overcome difficult times and move into a life of joy and happiness!

Christie Melonson

Christie Melonson is a psychotherapist, consultant, and educator on matters of diversity and transformation. She is a doctoral candidate in education with a concentration in organizational leadership and is a leader in a large mental health organization in Texas. Her professional interests include promoting positive personal and organizational change, advocating for victims of discrimination and abuse, and promoting diversity awareness in organizations. Christie's mission as a psychotherapist and consultant is to make the impossible possible and to help people grow so they can reach their goals. For more information, please visit her website at: http://christiemelonsonlpc.vpweb.com/.

Scott Edmund Miller

Scott Edmund Miller is the author of the self-help book *The User's Guide to Being Human: The Art and Science of Self*, which received the 2012 International Book Award for Best New Self-Help Book and the 2012 Next Generation Indie Book Award for Motivational Book of the Year. Scott is the author of a coming-of-age novel as well, *The Barefoot Warrior*, which he published under the pen name Kyle Weaver. He is co-founder of the 2009 California Public Charter School of the Year, an honor bestowed by the California Charter Schools Association.

Gloria Piantek

Gloria Piantek is an educational consultant with a master's degree in reading and special education from DePaul University. She has worked as a learning disabilities specialist, early childhood curriculum coordinator, Title I school coordinator, reading/language arts specialist, and special education teacher in Princeton, New Jersey, and Illinois. She has designed educational prescriptive/diagnostic techniques, presented at a New Jersey Education Association convention, and published an article on innovative teaching methods in the National Association of Secondary School Principals Bulletin.

Her interest in creative food preparation has produced hundreds of published recipes that have been selected as winners by various companies and competitions. She has appeared on television and radio and was selected as one of twenty finalists in the Next Greatest Speaker and Author competition. She lives with her husband in West Lafayette, Indiana.

Tianna Roser

Tianna Roser is a Reiki master teacher and certified clinical hypnotist specializing in emotional well-being and spiritual development. As the founder of Awakening Transformation, Tianna's mission is to empower individuals to experience their true selves, the source of genuine healing and growth. Tianna currently resides in Texas, where she aspires to "Keep Austin Weird." Learn more about Tianna by visiting her website at: www.awakeningtransfor mation.com.

books that inspire your body, mind, and spirit

Hierophant Publishing
8301 Broadway, Suite 219
San Antonio, TX 78209
888-800-4240

www.hierophantpublishing.com

Janet Rozzi

Janet Rozzi graduated with a bachelor's degree in marketing from Pennsylvania State University and has worked in sales for more than fifteen years.

She has published poetry but now focuses on writing non-fiction. She lives in Harrisburg, Pennsylvania, with her husband and three dogs.

Susana M. Silverhøj

Susana M. Silverhøj, master of social science and education, is a holistic heart intelligence coach, author, senior lecturer, and awakened business consultant. She co-founded the Holistic Life Academy and currently offers coaching, web courses, web TV, events, and retreats for families and individuals around the world. Her passion is helping overwhelmed and frustrated seekers and their children lead a conscious, healthy, and extraordinary life by creating balance between body, mind, heart, and soul. Her purpose in life is to help us see who we really are, feel good about life, and reconnect us all. She is a joyful and proud mother of three. Find out more at: holisticlifeacademy.com or email: susana@lifeacademy.com.

Nancy Smith

Nancy Smith is a psychic medium trained in the spiritualist tradition. She also practices energy healing and Peruvian healing techniques. Nancy strongly believes that the gift of mediumship is focused on helping those dealing with loss and grief to find some sense of healing, and she uses it as a healing modality to expand people's awareness about the continuity of their own lives. As an artist, Nancy's goal is to prove the continuity of life through her artwork. She is able to show a likeness of the communicator in a spirit drawing with pencil and pastel on paper. Nancy is currently teaching mediumship and spiritual development classes in her office and at the First Spiritualist Church of Quincy, Massachusetts. Nancy has two children and two stepchildren and lives happily ever after with her husband, Cort, and their dog, Rose.

Cliff Thomas

Cliff Thomas, MD, is a dad, surgeon, entrepreneur, author, and lover of life. He grew up in a small town in western Texas in the wild bell-bottom days of the seventies. Mentored by an uncle in the medical field who had a true passion for healing, Cliff decided to use his skills to help change lives and heal. He is now a leader in the areas of weight-loss surgery and esophageal-reflux surgery and has written two books on the subjects for patients. Writing these books sparked a desire to share what he has learned from divorce and relationships, and currently he is working on two self-help books on this topic. Cliff is single and his three kids are well on their way to being productive adults. To learn more, please visit: http://divorce formenwithintegrity.com or http://drcliffthomas.com.

Carole J Toms ND

Carole J Toms ND is a writer and qualified naturopath and homeopath with more than forty-five years of experience inspiring people to become all that they can be. Her book *How to Interpret Your Dreams: Knowing Your Dream Meanings* is due for release in early 2013 and will be available on her website, www.thedreamspecialist.com. Her motto is *"You are FAR GREATER than you imagine. Be INSPIRED to EVOLVE and CONNECT TO YOUR GREATNESS!"* She lives in southeast Queensland, Australia, with her wonderful husband.

Ann White

Ann White is a rabbi and trauma chaplain at a Level II trauma center in St. Petersburg, Florida. She is formerly a board-certified marital and family attorney and management consultant. She is the author of *Living with Spirit Energy* and *The Sacred Art of Dog Walking: Making the Ordinary Extraordinary* and a contributor to *Pebbles in the Pond: Transforming the World One Person at a Time.* The founder of Creating Calm within Chaos and the developer of Stress Rx for Medical Heroes, Ann also hosts a weekly Blog TalkRadio program called *Creating Calm* and serves on GoGreen Healthcare's advisory board. Her passions are wellness, creating inner calm, personal responsibility, and acts of kindness to bring peace into our lives and world. She advocates for animal rescue and leaving a small environmental footprint. You can find her at: www .creatingcalmwithinchaos.com.

Linda Wheeler Williams

Linda Wheeler Williams is a life coach and writer who guides and inspires others through coaching, teaching, and writing. Her approach is powerful, heartfelt, and engaging. At an early age, Linda felt that she was not heard and therefore discovered that her most effective form of communication was writing. Linda continues her journey of discovery by serving others. She currently resides in Phoenix, Arizona.